KB236430

초등 영어 논픽션 독해

저자

주선이

영어교육과 스토리텔링을 전공하고, 20여 년간 학생들을 지도하며 천재교육, 언어세상, 사회평론, YBM시사, NE능률 등 다수의 출판사와 영어 교재를 집필했다. 전통적인 영어교수법을 다양한 매체와 접목한 영어 프로그램을 기획 · 개발하고 있다.

대표 저서

〈초등 영어를 결정하는 파닉스〉, 〈초등 영어 처음 독해〉, 〈기적의 영어문장 만들기〉, 〈기적의 문법 + 영작〉, 〈기적의 동사 변화 트레이닝〉, 〈기적의 영어 문장 트레이닝〉, 〈바빠 영어 시제 특강〉, 〈맛있는 Everyday 초등 영문법〉, 〈가장 쉬운 초등 영어일기 따라쓰기〉 등

블로그

Sunny English Garden (https://blog.naver.com/sunyijoo)

초등 영어
논픽션 독해

저자 주선이
초판 1쇄 인쇄 2025년 8월 12일
초판 1쇄 발행 2025년 8월 22일

발행인 박효상　**편집장** 김현　**기획 · 편집** 장경희, 오혜순, 이한경, 박지행
디자인 임정현　**마케팅** 이태호, 이전희　**관리** 김태옥
표지 · 내지 디자인 김민정　**교정 · 교열 진행** 홍윤영
종이 월드페이퍼　**인쇄 · 제본** 예림인쇄 · 바인딩　**녹음** YR미디어

출판등록 제10-1835호　**발행처** 사람in
주소 04034 서울시 마포구 양화로 11길 14-10(서교동) 3F
전화 02) 338-3555(代)　**팩스** 02) 338-3545
E-mail saramin@netsgo.com　**Website** www.saramin.com

책값은 뒤표지에 있습니다. 파본은 바꾸어 드립니다.

ⓒ 주선이 2025

ISBN
979-11-7101-174-2 64740
978-89-6049-808-2 (set)

우아한 지적만보, 기민한 실사구시 사람in

어린이제품안전특별법에 의한 제품표시		
KC	**제조자명** 사람in **제조국명** 대한민국 **사용연령** 5세 이상 어린이 제품	**전화번호** 02-338-3555 **주　소** 서울시 마포구 양화로 11길 14-10 3층

초등 영어 논픽션 독해

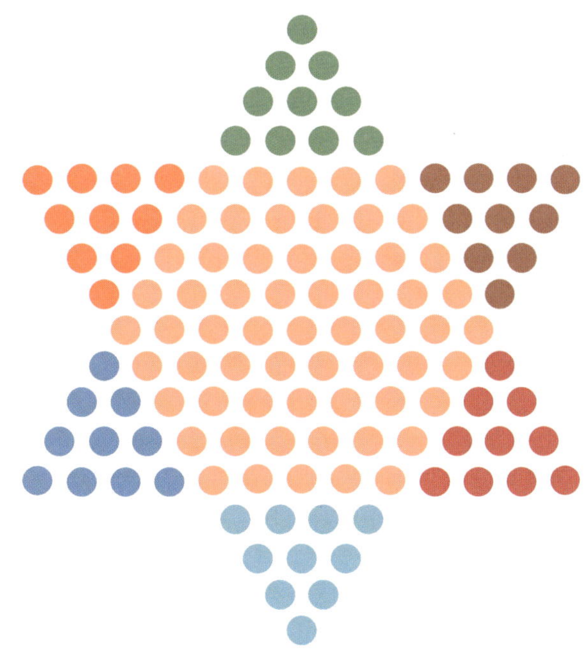

사람in

논픽션(nonfiction, 비문학) 정독·다독을 위한 읽기 전략을 배워요.

<초등 영어 논픽션 독해>는 초등 고학년이나 예비 중등생을 위한 영어 읽기 훈련서예요. 과학적인 사실에 근거한, 정보 전달을 목적으로 하는 지문을 바탕으로 정독(intensive reading)과 다독(extensive reading)을 위한 효율적인 독서 방법을 알려주고자 기획되었어요.

아무리 자세히 반복해서 읽어도 글의 내용을 제대로 이해하지 못하면 질문에 대한 답을 찾을 수 없어요. 그래서 제한된 시간 안에 글을 빠르게 읽는 연습이 함께 이루어져야 해요. 짧은 시간 안에 전체적인 맥락을 빠르게 파악하여 그 안에서 중요한 정보를 가려낼 수 있도록 하기 위해서죠.

이 책은 빨리 읽고 정확히 이해할 수 있도록 다음 4가지 효과적인 읽기 전략과 실전 활동들로 구성되어 있어요.

읽기 전략 1 주제별 어휘를 배우고, 영영 풀이 익히기

주제별 어휘를 분류·정리하는 습관을 갖도록 해요. 단어의 정의(definition)를 영어로 익히면 관련 어휘 실력도 늘고, 구체적이고 자연스러운 영어식 표현을 배울 수 있어요.

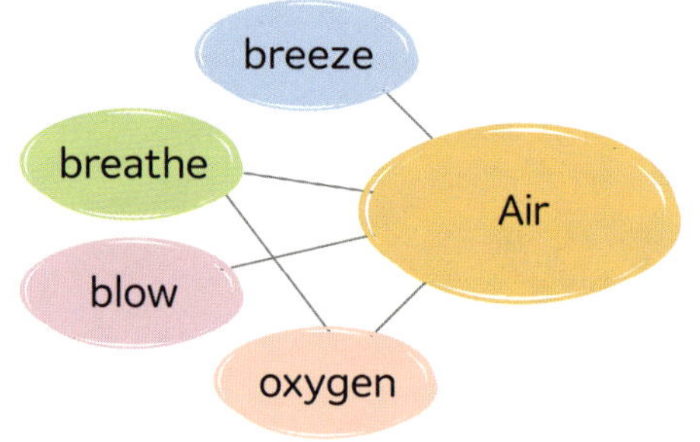

단어 모둠(Word Cluster)을 이용하여 주제별 단어 시각화

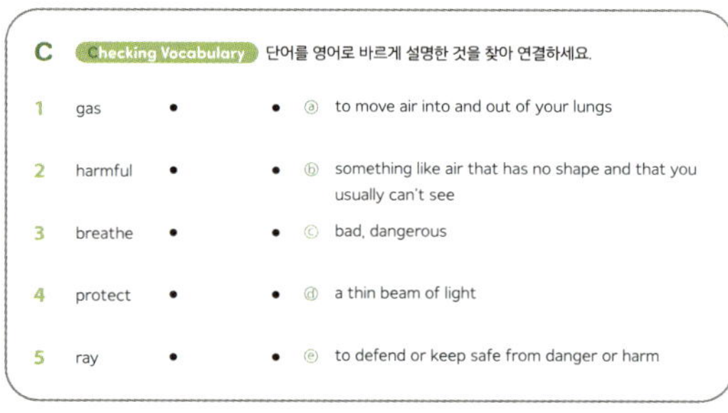

단어 정의의 영영 풀이 익히기

읽기 전략 2 의미 덩어리(청크)로 끊어 읽기

단어를 보다 큰 그룹인 의미 덩어리로 끊어 읽으면 시선을 빠르게 이동하여 읽기 속도를 높일 수 있고, 뇌의 정보 처리 부담을 줄여서 더 잘 이해하고 오래 기억할 수 있어요. 또, 자연스럽게 영어 어순을 배우게 도와 긴 문장도 빠르고 정확하게 직독 직해가 가능해지죠.

By day, / air protects us / from harmful rays / from the sun.

빠른 읽기와 이해를 돕는 청킹(chunking) 연습

 목적에 필요한 부분만 집중해서 빠르게 읽기

처음에는 지문을 빠르게 읽으면서 중심어를 기준으로 전체적인 맥락과 핵심을 파악해요. 그리고 필요한 특정 정보를 찾으려 글을 다시 읽으면 세부 내용까지 파악할 수 있어요.

빠르게 훑어 읽기(스키밍: skimming)

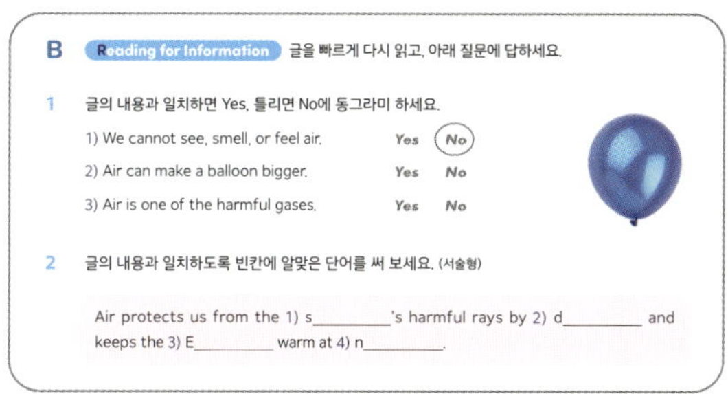

답 찾아 읽기(스캐닝: scanning)

 모든 지문을 완전히 이해하기 위해 자세히 읽기

의미 덩어리로 나뉜 내용을 자세하게 읽으며 문장의 구조를 파악하고, 각 문장에 적용된 문법 요소와 구체적인 세부 사항을 확인해요. 이후 다시 자세히 읽으며 영문장 구조와 문법도 학습해요.

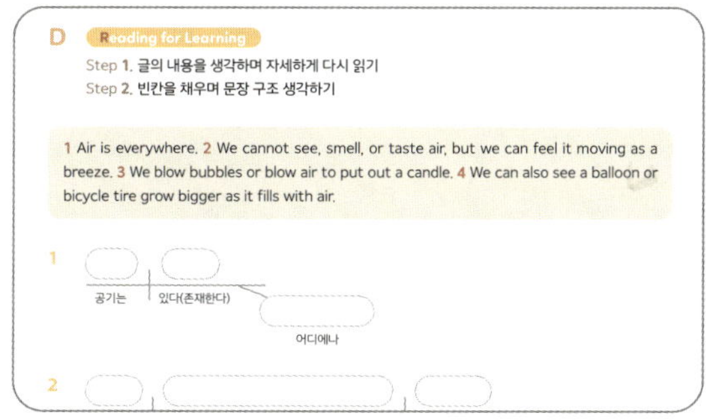

직독 직해를 위한 끊어(청킹) 읽기

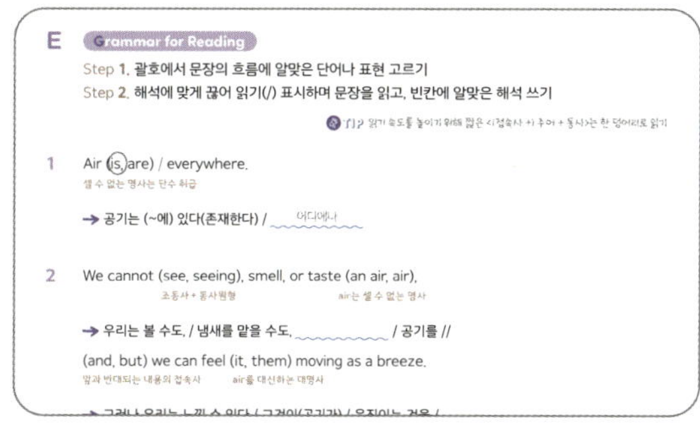

독해에 필요한 핵심 문법 정리하기

이 책이 논픽션 독해로 첫걸음을 내딛는 학습자들을 즐겁고 의미 있는 독서의 세계로 이끄는 든든한 디딤돌이 되기를 바랍니다.

주선이

이 책의 구성 및 특징

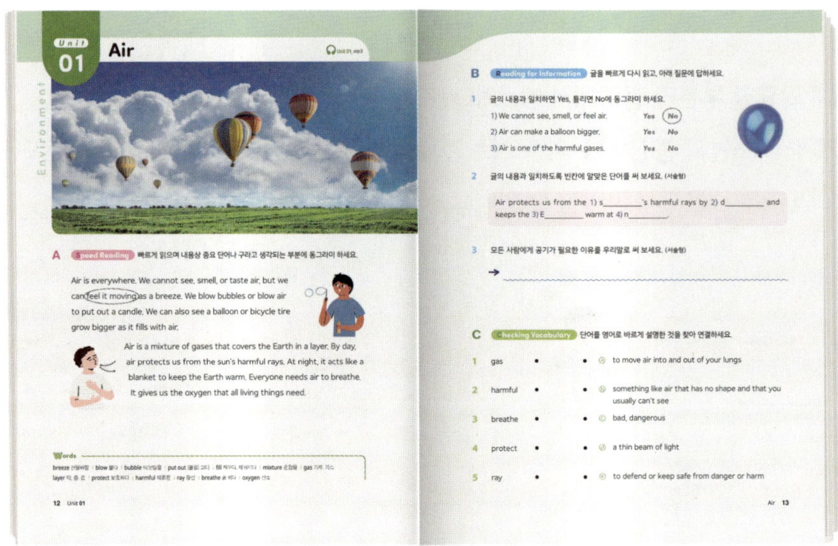

A **Speed Reading**

다양한 주제의 지문을 읽으며 지식을 확장합니다.
원어민 녹음을 들으며 듣기 실력도 키웁니다.

B **Reading for Information**

지문을 제대로 이해하고 있는지 여러 가지 문제를 통해
확인하며 내용을 정리합니다.

C **Checking Vocabulary**

단어의 영영 해설을 통해 중요 단어의 의미까지 제대로
이해하고 있는지 확인합니다.

문장 구조 해부 미리 알아두기

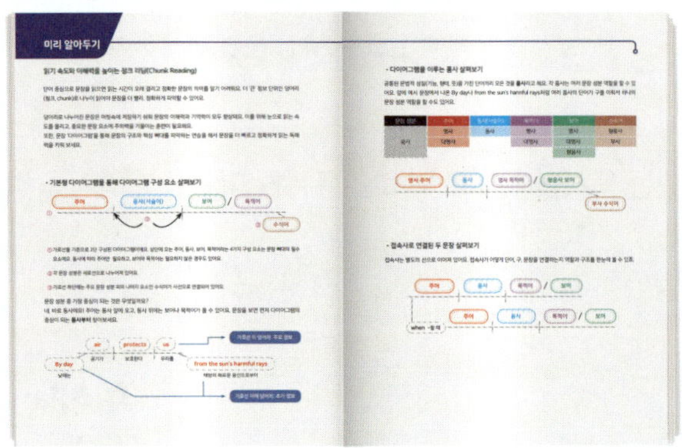

정답 및 해석

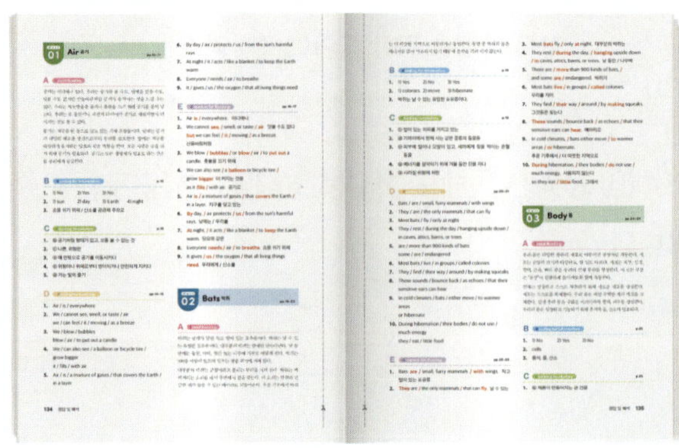

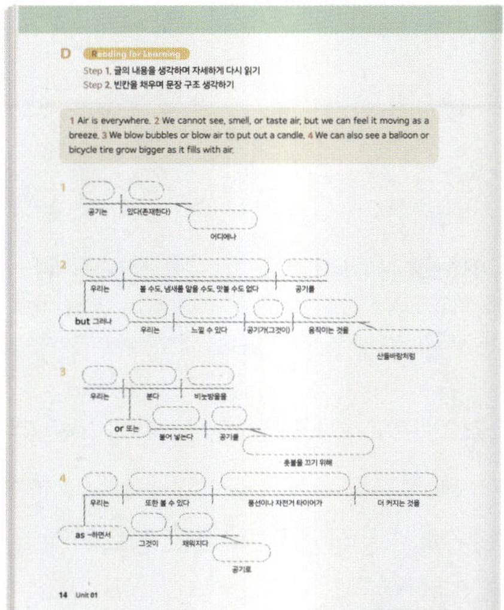

D Reading for Learning

지문을 다시 읽고 문장을 해부하면서 어떤 구조로
영어 문장이 구성되었는지 파악합니다.

E Grammar for Reading

문장을 끊어 읽으며 해석할 수 있도록 연습해 읽기
실력을 올립니다. 주요 문법 사항 설명을 보며 영문장의
기본 문법 실력도 키웁니다.

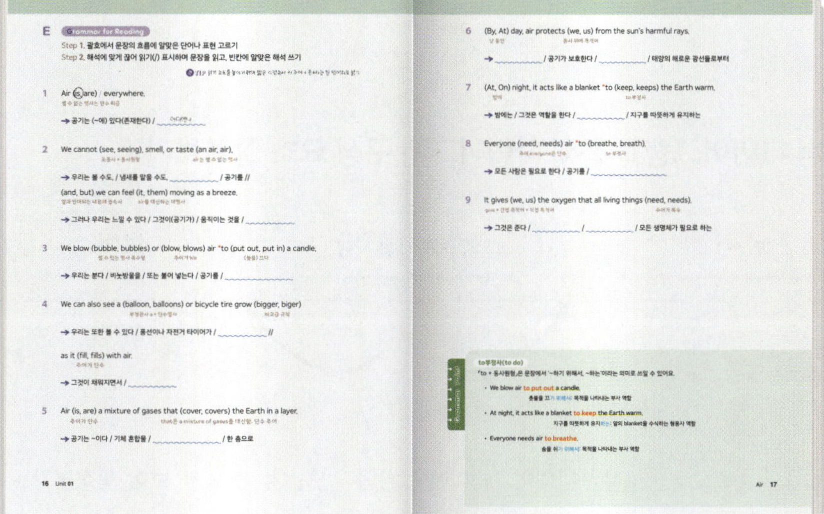

원어민 녹음 듣기

QR코드를 스캔하면
이 책의 자료실이 바로 나옵니다.

• 각 Unit 지문 MP3 파일: 위에 QR코드를 스캔하면
전체 파일을 다운로드 받거나 바로 들을 수 있습니다.
▶ 바로듣기 를 탭하면 파일 목록이 나오고, 이때 원하
는 파일을 선택해 들을 수 있습니다. 재생속도 조절과
반복 듣기도 가능합니다.

• 홈페이지 saramin.com ▶ 도서명 검색
• 네이버 [오디오클립] ▶ 도서명 검색

단어 목록, 단어 테스트

• 사람in 홈페이지(www.saramin.com)에서 단어장과
단어 테스트지를 다운로드 받을 수 있습니다.

읽기 속도와 이해력을 높이는 청크 리딩(Chunk Reading)

단어 중심으로 문장을 읽으면 읽는 시간이 오래 걸리고 정확한 문장의 의미를 알기 어려워요. 더 '큰' 정보 단위인 덩어리(청크, chunk)로 나누어 읽어야 문장을 더 빨리, 정확하게 파악할 수 있어요.

덩어리로 나누어진 문장은 머릿속에 저장하기 쉬워 문장의 이해력과 기억력이 모두 향상돼요. 이를 위해 눈으로 읽는 속도를 올리고, 중요한 문장 요소에 주의력을 기울이는 훈련이 필요해요.
또한, 문장 '다이어그램'을 통해 문장의 구조와 핵심 뼈대를 파악하는 연습을 해서 문장을 더 빠르고 정확하게 읽는 독해력을 키워 보세요.

• 기본형 다이어그램을 통해 다이어그램 구성 요소 살펴보기

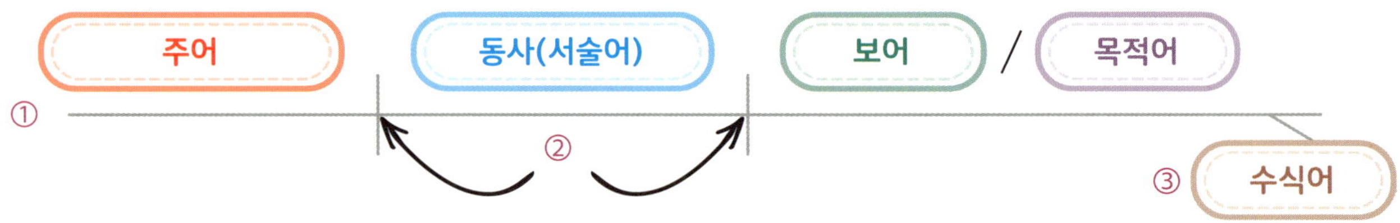

① 가로선을 기준으로 2단 구성된 다이어그램이에요. 상단에 오는 주어, 동사, 보어, 목적어라는 4가지 구성 요소는 문장 뼈대의 필수 요소예요. 동사에 따라 주어만 필요하고, 보어와 목적어는 필요하지 않은 경우도 있어요.

② 각 문장 성분은 세로선으로 나누어져 있어요.

③ 가로선 하단에는 주요 문장 성분 외의 나머지 요소인 수식어가 사선으로 연결되어 있어요.

문장 성분 중 가장 중심이 되는 것은 무엇일까요?
네, 바로 동사예요! 주어는 동사 앞에 오고, 동사 뒤에는 보어나 목적어가 올 수 있어요. 문장을 보면 먼저 다이어그램의 중심이 되는 **동사부터** 찾아보세요.

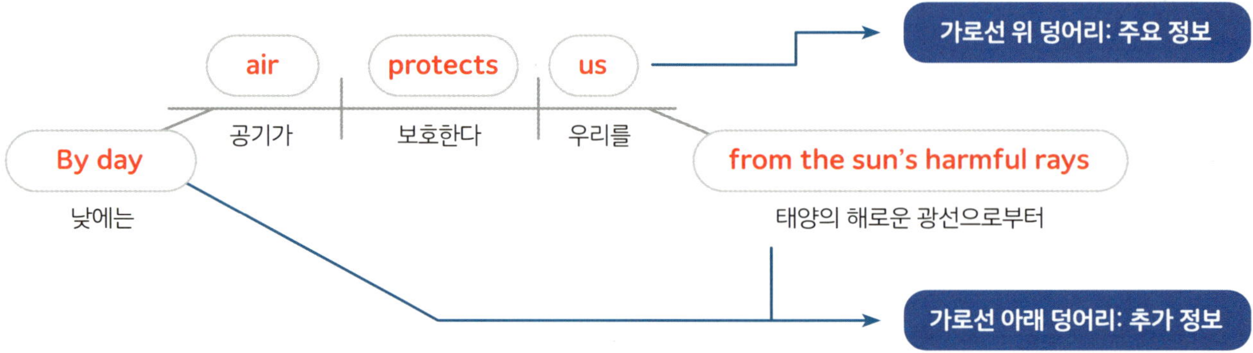

• 다이어그램을 이루는 품사 살펴보기

공통된 문법적 성질(기능, 형태, 뜻)을 가진 단어끼리 모은 것을 **품사**라고 해요. 각 품사는 여러 문장 성분 역할을 할 수 있어요. 앞에 예시 문장에서 나온 By day나 from the sun's harmful rays처럼 여러 품사의 단어가 구를 이뤄서 하나의 문장 성분 역할을 할 수도 있어요.

문장 성분	주어	동사(서술어)	목적어	보어	수식어
품사	명사	동사	명사	명사	형용사
	대명사		대명사	대명사	부사
				형용사	

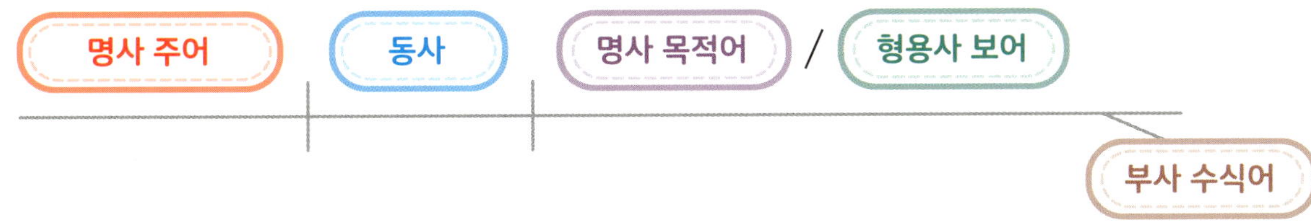

• 접속사로 연결된 두 문장 살펴보기

접속사는 별도의 선으로 이어져 있어요. 접속사가 어떻게 단어, 구, 문장을 연결하는지 역할과 구조를 한눈에 볼 수 있죠.

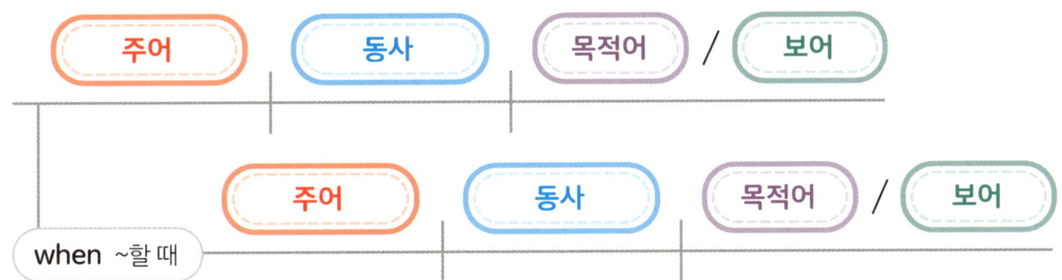

차례

Let's
begin!

Unit 01 — Air

A **Speed Reading** 빠르게 읽으며 내용상 중요 단어나 구라고 생각되는 부분에 동그라미 하세요.

Air is everywhere. We cannot see, smell, or taste air, but we can feel it moving as a breeze. We blow bubbles or blow air to put out a candle. We can also see a balloon or bicycle tire grow bigger as it fills with air.

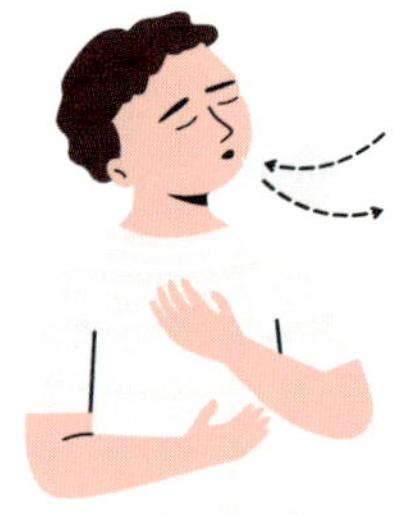

Air is a mixture of gases that covers the Earth in a layer. By day, air protects us from the sun's harmful rays. At night, it acts like a blanket to keep the Earth warm. Everyone needs air to breathe. It gives us the oxygen that all living things need.

Words

breeze 산들바람 ∣ blow 불다 ∣ bubble 비눗방울 ∣ put out (불을) 끄다 ∣ fill 채우다, 채워지다 ∣ mixture 혼합물 ∣ gas 기체, 가스
layer 막, 층, 겹 ∣ protect 보호하다 ∣ harmful 해로운 ∣ ray 광선 ∣ breathe 숨 쉬다 ∣ oxygen 산소

1 글의 내용과 일치하면 Yes, 틀리면 No에 동그라미 하세요.

1) We cannot see, smell, or feel air.   Yes   (No)

2) Air can make a balloon bigger.   Yes   No

3) Air is one of the harmful gases.   Yes   No

2 글의 내용과 일치하도록 빈칸에 알맞은 단어를 써 보세요. (서술형)

Air protects us from the 1) s__________'s harmful rays by 2) d__________ and keeps the 3) E__________ warm at 4) n__________.

3 모든 사람에게 공기가 필요한 이유를 우리말로 써 보세요. (서술형)

➜ ____

C **Checking Vocabulary** 단어를 영어로 바르게 설명한 것을 찾아 연결하세요.

1 gas   ●   ● ⓐ to move air into and out of your lungs

2 harmful   ●   ● ⓑ something like air that has no shape and that you usually can't see

3 breathe   ●   ● ⓒ bad, dangerous

4 protect   ●   ● ⓓ a thin beam of light

5 ray   ●   ● ⓔ to defend or keep safe from danger or harm

Step **1.** 글의 내용을 생각하며 자세하게 다시 읽기
Step **2.** 빈칸을 채우며 문장 구조 생각하기

1 Air is everywhere. **2** We cannot see, smell, or taste air, but we can feel it moving as a breeze. **3** We blow bubbles or blow air to put out a candle. **4** We can also see a balloon or bicycle tire grow bigger as it fills with air.

5 Air is a mixture of gases that covers the Earth in a layer. **6** By day, air protects us from the sun's harmful rays. **7** At night, it acts like a blanket to keep the Earth warm. **8** Everyone needs air to breathe. **9** It gives us the oxygen that all living things need.

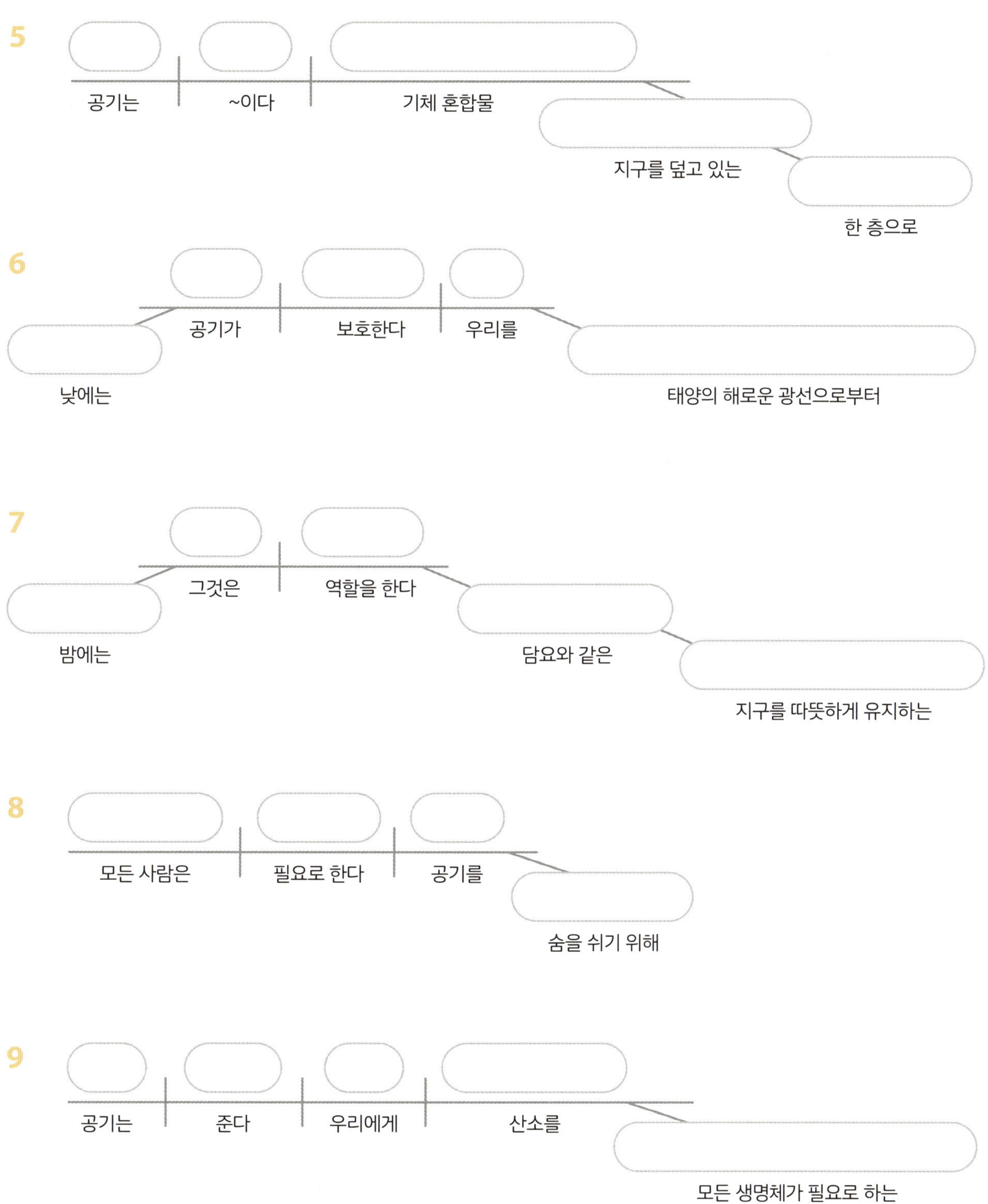

Step **1.** 괄호에서 문장의 흐름에 알맞은 단어나 표현 고르기
Step **2.** 해석에 맞게 끊어 읽기(/) 표시하며 문장을 읽고, 빈칸에 알맞은 해석 쓰기

TIP 읽기 속도를 높이기 위해 짧은 <(접속사 +) 주어 + 동사>는 한 덩어리로 읽기

1 Air (is, are) / everywhere.
셀 수 없는 명사는 단수 취급

→ 공기는 (~에) 있다(존재한다) / ______어디에나______

2 We cannot (see, seeing), smell, or taste (an air, air),
          조동사 + 동사원형   air는 셀 수 없는 명사

→ 우리는 볼 수도, / 냄새를 맡을 수도, ____________ / 공기를 //

(and, but) we can feel (it, them) moving as a breeze.
앞과 반대되는 내용의 접속사   air를 대신하는 대명사

→ 그러나 우리는 느낄 수 있다 / 그것이(공기가) / 움직이는 것을 / ____________

3 We blow (bubble, bubbles) or (blow, blows) air *to (put out, put in) a candle.
          셀 수 있는 명사 복수형   주어가 We   (불을) 끄다

→ 우리는 분다 / 비눗방울을 / 또는 불어 넣는다 / 공기를 / ____________

4 We can also see a (balloon, balloons) or bicycle tire grow (bigger, biger)
              부정관사 a + 단수명사   비교급 규칙

→ 우리는 또한 볼 수 있다 / 풍선이나 자전거 타이어가 / ____________ //

as it (fill, fills) with air.
      주어가 단수

→ 그것이 채워지면서 / ____________

5 Air (is, are) a mixture of gases that (cover, covers) the Earth in a layer.
      주어가 단수   that은 a mixture of gases를 대신함. 단수 주어

→ 공기는 ~이다 / 기체 혼합물 / ____________ / 한 층으로

6 (By, At) day, air protects (we, us) from the sun's harmful rays.
낮 동안   동사 뒤에 목적어

→ ___________ / 공기가 보호한다 / ___________ / 태양의 해로운 광선들로부터

7 (At, On) night, it acts like a blanket *to (keep, keeps) the Earth warm.
밤에   to 부정사

→ 밤에는 / 그것은 역할을 한다 / ___________ / 지구를 따뜻하게 유지하는

8 Everyone (need, needs) air *to (breathe, breath).
주어 everyone은 단수   to 부정사

→ 모든 사람은 필요로 한다 / 공기를 / ___________

9 It gives (we, us) the oxygen that all living things (need, needs).
give + 간접 목적어 + 직접 목적어   주어가 복수

→ 그것은 준다 / ___________ / ___________ / 모든 생명체가 필요로 하는

to부정사(to do)

「to + 동사원형」은 문장에서 '~하기 위해서, ~하는'이라는 의미로 쓰일 수 있어요.

- We blow air **to put out** a candle.
  촛불을 끄기 위해서: 목적을 나타내는 부사 역할

- At night, it acts like a blanket **to keep** the Earth warm.
  지구를 따뜻하게 유지하는: 앞의 blanket을 수식하는 형용사 역할

- Everyone needs air **to breathe**.
  숨을 쉬기 위해서: 목적을 나타내는 부사 역할

Unit 02

Bats

Unit 02_mp3

A **Speed Reading** 빠르게 읽으며 내용상 중요 단어나 구라고 생각되는 부분에 동그라미 하세요.

Bats are small, furry mammals with wings. They are the only mammals that can fly. Most bats fly only at night. They rest during the day, hanging upside down in caves, attics, barns, or trees. There are more than 900 kinds of bats, and some are endangered.

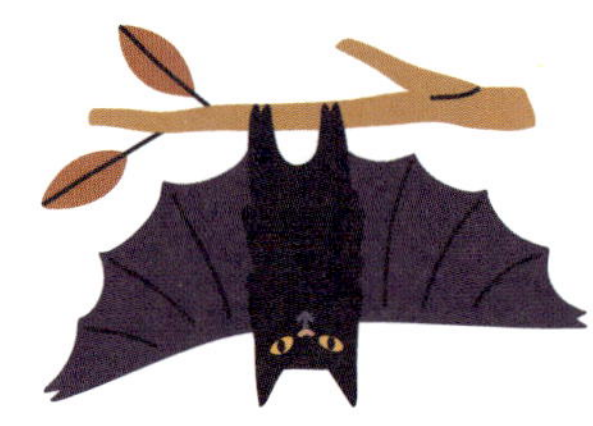

Most bats live in groups called colonies. They find their way around by making squeaks. These sounds bounce back as echoes that their sensitive ears can hear. In cold climates, bats either move to warmer areas or hibernate. During hibernation, their bodies do not use much energy, so they eat little food.

Words

furry 털로 덮인 | mammal 포유류 | rest 쉬다 | attic 다락방 | barn 헛간 | endangered 멸종 위기에 처한 | colony 군집
squeak 찍찍 우는 소리 | bounce 반사하다, 튀어 오르다 | echo 메아리 | sensitive 민감한 | hibernate 동면하다 (hibernation 동면)

1 글의 내용과 일치하면 Yes, 틀리면 No에 동그라미 하세요.

1) Bats are not birds.　　　　　　　　　**Yes**　　**No**

2) Bats cannot fly at night.　　　　　　　**Yes**　　**No**

3) Bats have sensitive ears.　　　　　　　**Yes**　　**No**

2 글의 내용과 일치하도록 빈칸에 알맞은 단어를 써 보세요. (서술형)

Most bats live in groups called 1) c__________. They 2) m__________ to warmer areas or 3) h__________ in cold climates.

3 박쥐가 다른 포유류와 다른 점을 우리말로 써 보세요. (서술형)

→ ____

C **Checking Vocabulary** 단어를 영어로 바르게 설명한 것을 찾아 연결하세요.

1 furry　　　　　　　ⓐ in danger of disappearing

2 colony　　　　　　ⓑ to sleep through the winter to save energy

3 mammal　　　　　ⓒ having a coat of fur

4 hibernate　　　　ⓓ animals of the same type living closely together

5 endangered　　　ⓔ a warm-blooded animal that has fur or hair on its skin and feeds milk to its babies

Step **1.** 글의 내용을 생각하며 자세하게 다시 읽기
Step **2.** 빈칸을 채우며 문장 구조 생각하기

1 Bats are small, furry mammals with wings. **2** They are the only mammals that can fly. **3** Most bats fly only at night. **4** They rest during the day, hanging upside down in caves, attics, barns, or trees. **5** There are more than 900 kinds of bats, and some are endangered.

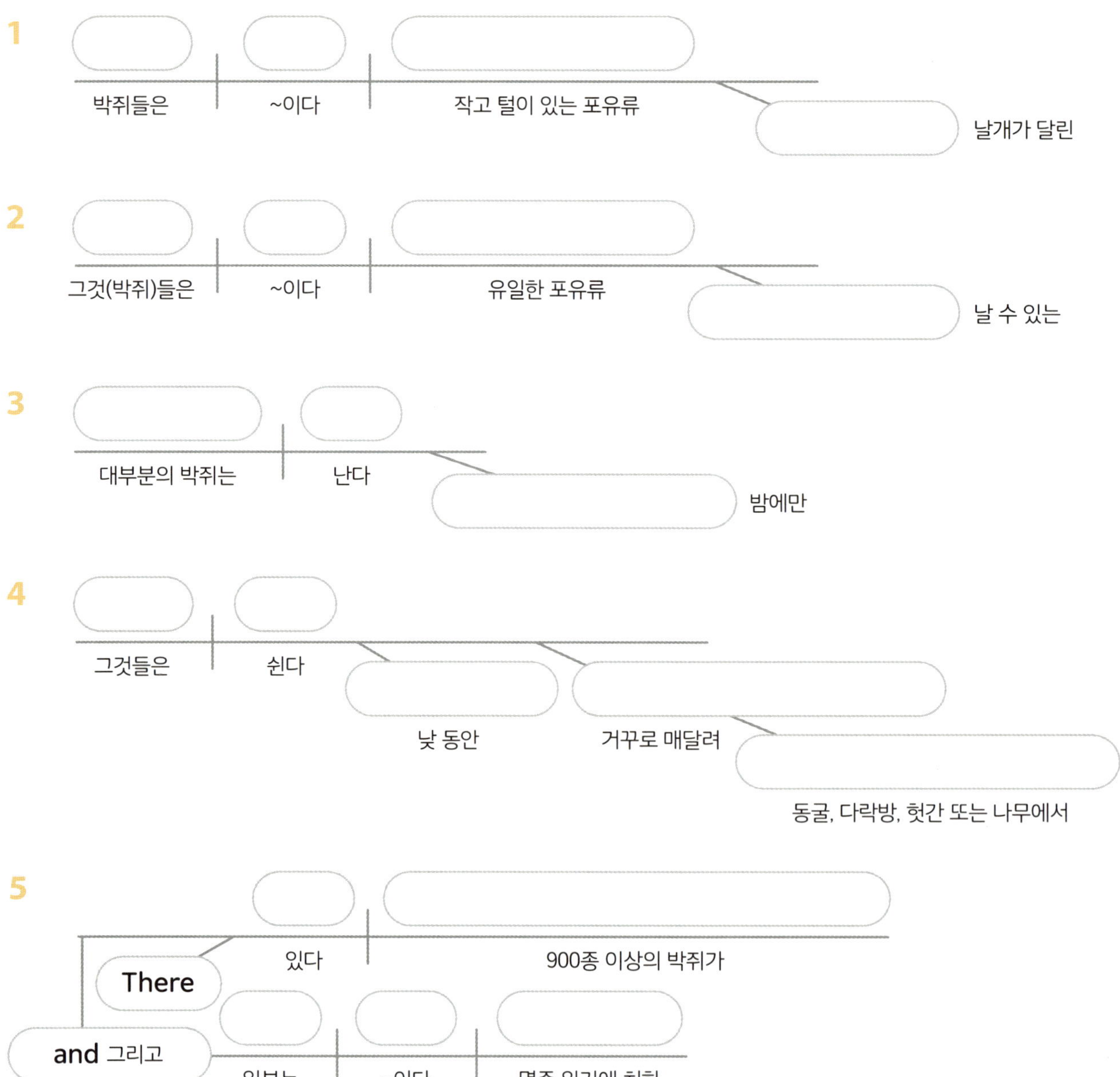

6 Most bats live in groups called colonies. **7** They find their way around by making squeaks. **8** These sounds bounce back as echoes that their sensitive ears can hear. **9** In cold climates, bats either move to warmer areas or hibernate. **10** During hibernation, their bodies do not use much energy, so they eat little food.

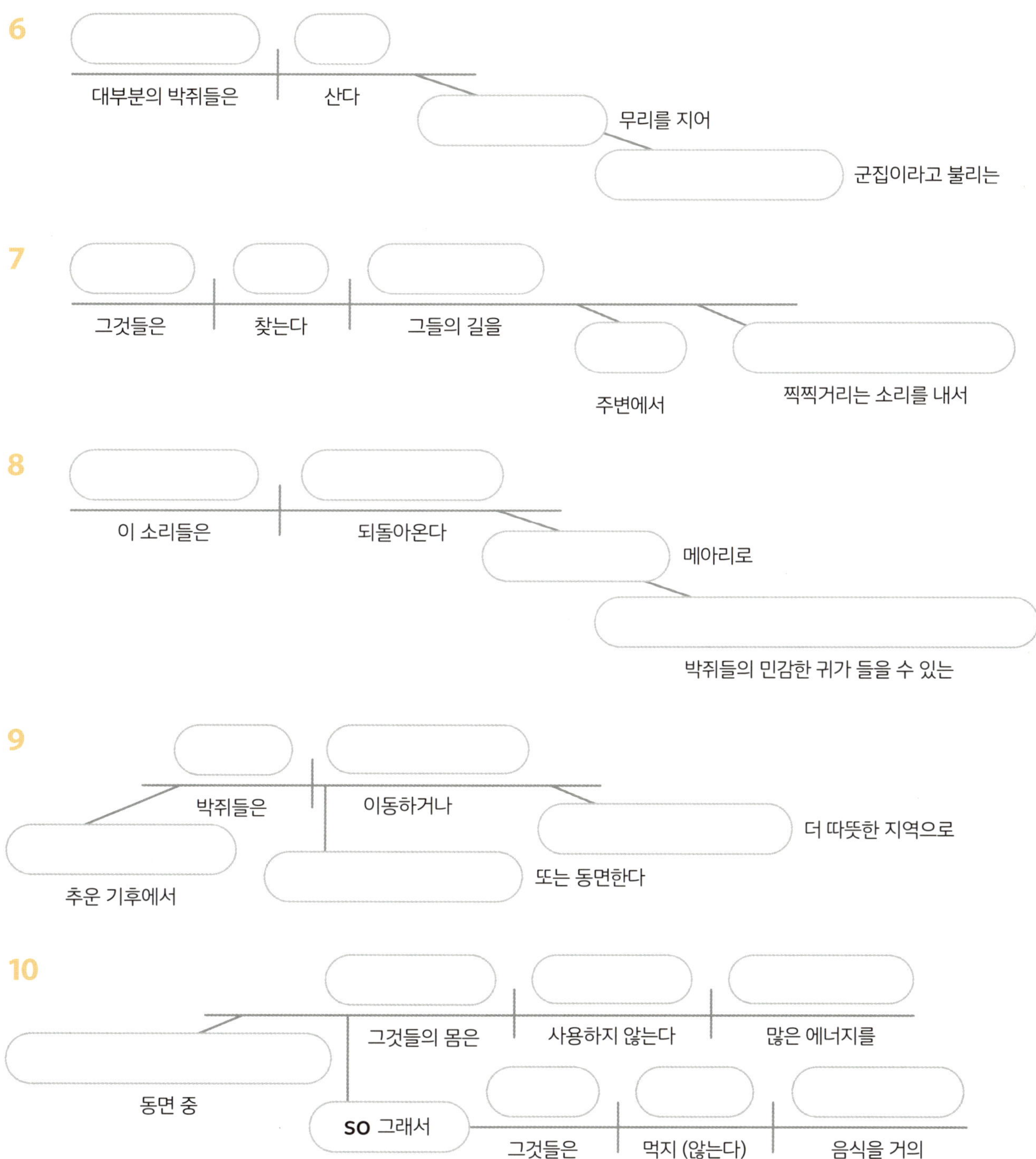

Step **1.** 괄호에서 문장의 흐름에 알맞은 단어나 표현 고르기
Step **2.** 해석에 맞게 끊어 읽기(/) 표시하며 문장을 읽고, 빈칸에 알맞은 해석 쓰기

TIP 읽기 속도를 높이기 위해 짧은 <(접속사 +) 주어 + 동사>는 한 덩어리로 읽기

1　Bats (is, are) small, furry mammals (with, by) wings.
　　　주어가 복수　　　　　　　　　　　　　　　~을 가지고 있는

→ 박쥐들은 ~이다 / ＿＿＿＿＿＿＿＿＿＿＿ / 날개가 달린

2　(It, They) are the only mammals *that can (fly, flies).
　　　Bats를 대신하는 대명사 주어　　　　　　　　조동사 + 동사원형

→ 그것들은 ~이다 / 유일한 포유류 / ＿＿＿＿＿＿＿＿

3　Most (bat, bats) fly only (at, in) night.
　　　most + 셀 수 있는 명사 복수형　　시간 전치사(~에)

→ ＿＿＿＿＿＿＿＿＿＿＿ 난다 / 밤에만

4　They rest (during, for) the day, (hang, hanging) upside down (in, at) caves,
　　　　　　　~ 동안　　　　　　　　분사구문(~하면서)　　　　　장소 전치사(~ 안에)

attics, barns, or trees.
→ 그것들은 쉰다 / ＿＿＿＿＿＿＿, / 거꾸로 매달려 / 동굴, 다락방, 헛간 또는 ＿＿＿＿＿＿

5　There are (more, many) than 900 kinds of bats, and some (are, is) endangered.
　　　　　　　　　than은 비교급과 함께　　　　　　　　　　some(일부 박쥐)이 주어

→ 있다 / 900종 이상의 ＿＿＿＿＿＿＿, / 그리고 일부는 ~이다 / 멸종 위기에 처한

6　Most bats (live, lives) in groups (call, called) colonies.
　　　주어가 복수　　　　　　　~라고 불리는

→ 대부분의 박쥐들은 산다 / ＿＿＿＿＿＿＿ / 군집이라고 불리는

7 They find (its, their) way around by (make, making) squeaks.
주어 They의 소유격　　　　　　전치사 by 뒤에는 동명사

→ ______________ / 그것들의 길을 / 주변에서 / 찍찍거리는 소리를 내어

8 (These, This) sounds bounce back as echoes that their sensitive ears can (hear, hears).
복수인 sounds를 수식　　　　　　　　　　　　　　조동사 + 동사원형

→ 이 소리들은 / 되돌아온다 / ______________ / 그것들의 민감한 귀가 들을 수 있는

9 In cold climates, bats either move (to, in) warmer areas (or, and) hibernate.
　　　　　　　　　　　　　~로　　　　　　　　또는

→ ______________ / 박쥐들은 이동하거나 / ______________ / 또는 동면한다

10 (During, After) hibernation, their bodies (do, does) not use (much, many) energy,
　　~ 동안　　　　　　　　　　주어가 복수　　　energy는 셀 수 없는 명사

→ 동면 중 / 그것들의 몸은 / ______________ / 많은 에너지를 //

so they eat (little, few) food.
food는 셀 수 없는 명사

→ ______________ 그것들은 먹지 (않는다) / 음식을 거의

관계대명사 that
두 문장을 하나로 만들 때 사용되는 관계대명사 that은 '저것'이라 해석하지 않고 두 문장을 이어주는 대명사 역할을 해요.
관계대명사가 들어간 문장은 '~하는'이라고 해석되어 형용사처럼 앞의 말을 수식해요.

- They(Bats) are the only mammals. + They(Bats) can fly.
  → They are the only mammals **that** can fly.

1) 두 문장을 하나로 만들기 위해 두 문장의 공통 요소인 Bats를 대신하는 뒷 문장의 주어 They를 생략해요.
2) 단어가 생략된 자리에는 관계대명사 that을 써요.
3) 뒤의 문장은 앞 문장 주어에 대한 추가적인 정보를 주는 역할로, '날 수 있는'이라고 해석해요.

Body

Health & Life

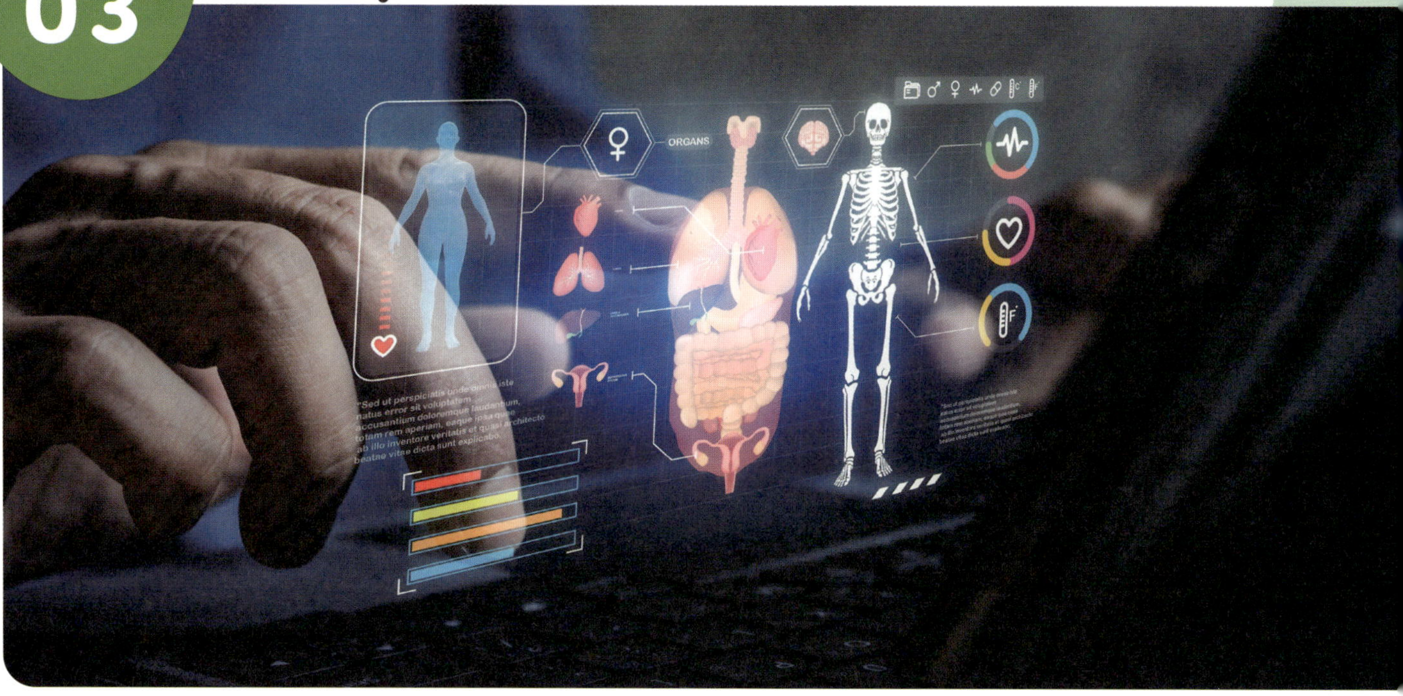

A **Speed Reading** 빠르게 읽으며 내용상 중요 단어나 구라고 생각되는 부분에 동그라미 하세요.

Our body works like a factory with many types of cells. The cells come in different shapes and sizes and have different jobs to do. They form the parts of our body, such as the skin, heart, blood, muscles, and bones. All these parts work together to keep the "factory" running smoothly.

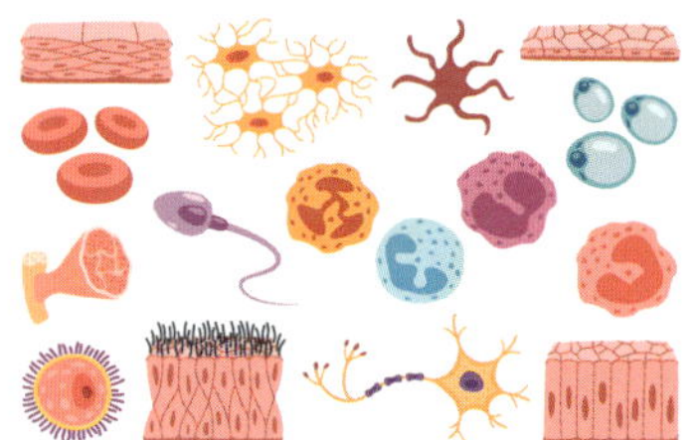

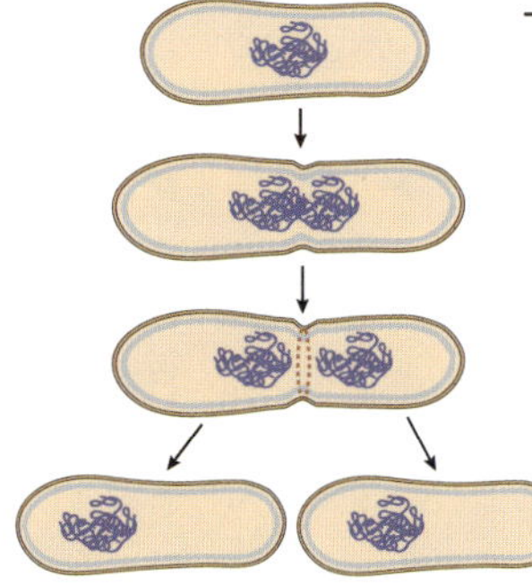

The human body creates new cells to grow and heal itself. Cells make copies of themselves. Our body replaces millions of cells every day. Over a lifetime, it produces a lot of hair, blood, and skin. Our body needs food, water, and oxygen to grow and function.

Words

factory 공장 ┃ cell 세포 ┃ form 구성하다 ┃ muscle 근육 ┃ smoothly 원활하게 ┃ create 생성하다 ┃ heal 치유하다 ┃ copy 복사본
replace 대체하다, 교체하다 ┃ millions of 수백만 개의 ┃ lifetime 평생 ┃ produce 생산하다 ┃ function 기능하다

1 글의 내용과 일치하면 Yes, 틀리면 No에 동그라미 하세요.

1) The human body has only one type of cell. **Yes** **No**

2) The body needs new cells to grow. **Yes** **No**

3) Our body replaces millions of bones every day. **Yes** **No**

2 글의 내용과 일치하도록 빈칸에 공통으로 들어갈 단어를 써 보세요. (서술형)

- The ___________ come in different shapes and sizes.
- The ___________ form the parts of your body.

3 신체가 성장하고 기능하기 위해 필요한 3가지를 우리말로 써 보세요. (서술형)

→ ____

C **C**hecking Vocabulary 단어를 영어로 바르게 설명한 것을 찾아 연결하세요.

1 factory • • ⓐ the soft pieces of flesh in animals and humans that make the bones move

2 muscles • • ⓑ a large building where products are made

3 heal • • ⓒ something that looks exactly like another thing

4 copy • • ⓓ the time during which a person is alive

5 lifetime • • ⓔ to become healthy or whole again

Step **1.** 글의 내용을 생각하며 자세하게 다시 읽기
Step **2.** 빈칸을 채우며 문장 구조 생각하기

1 Our body works like a factory with many types of cells. **2** The cells come in different shapes and sizes and have different jobs to do. **3** They form the parts of our body, such as the skin, heart, blood, muscles, and bones. **4** All these parts work together to keep the "factory" running smoothly.

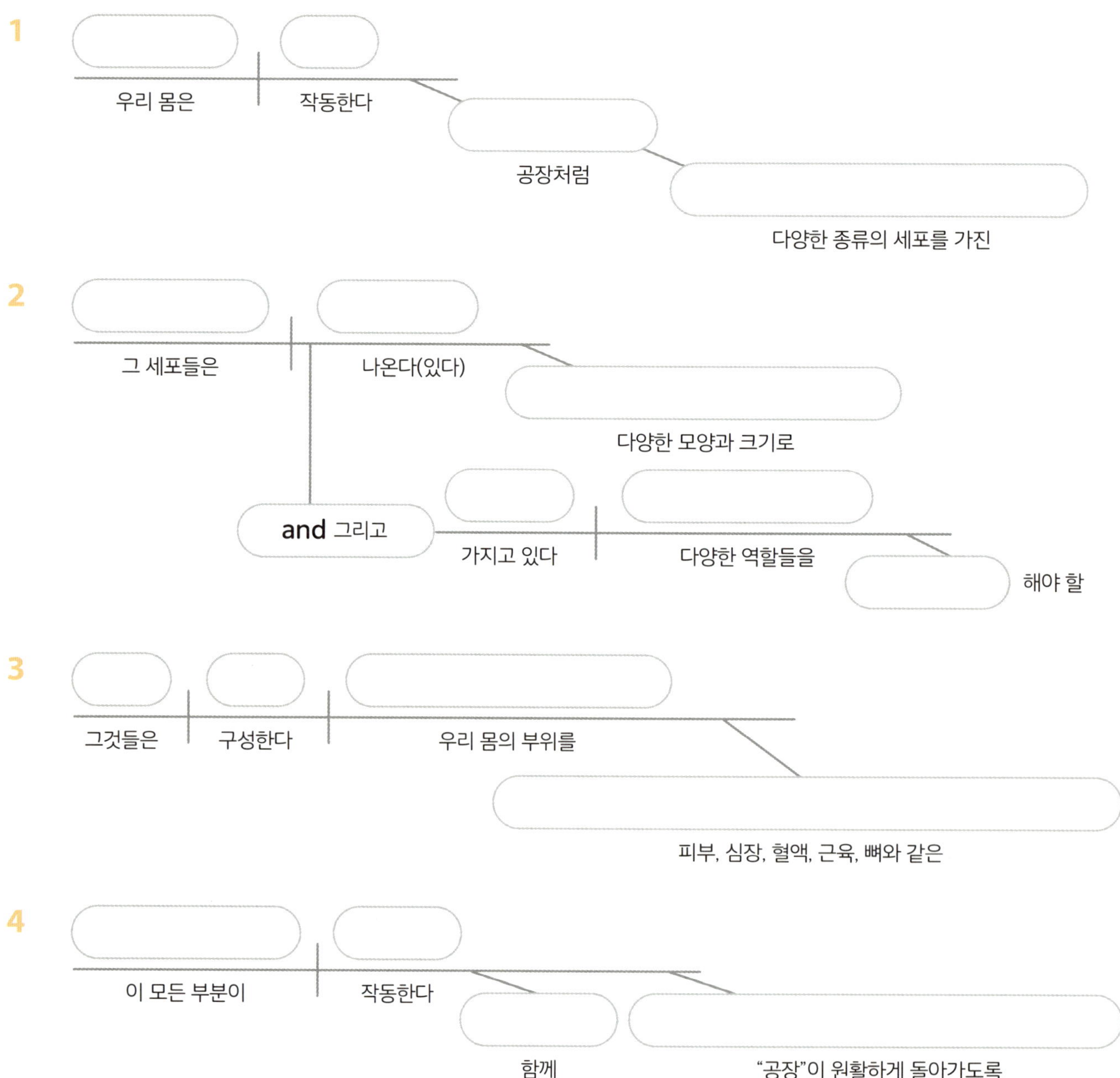

5 The human body creates new cells to grow and heal itself. **6** Cells make copies of themselves. **7** Our body replaces millions of cells every day. **8** Over a lifetime, it produces a lot of hair, blood, and skin. **9** Our body needs food, water, and oxygen to grow and function.

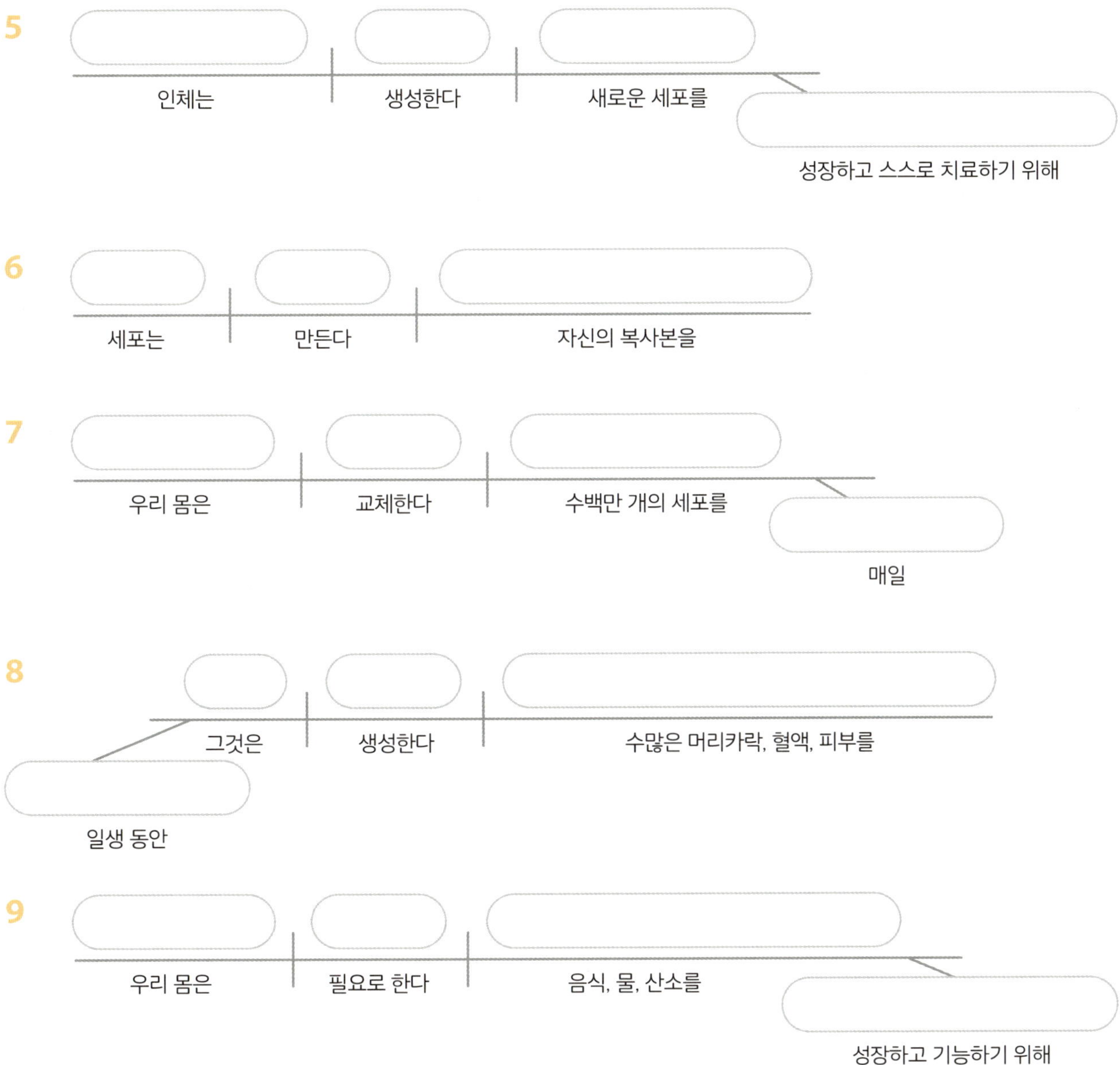

E **Grammar for Reading**

Step **1.** 괄호에서 문장의 흐름에 알맞은 단어나 표현 고르기
Step **2.** 해석에 맞게 끊어 읽기(/) 표시하며 문장을 읽고, 빈칸에 알맞은 해석 쓰기

TIP 읽기 속도를 높이기 위해 짧은 <(접속사 +) 주어 + 동사>는 한 덩어리로 읽기

1 Our body (work, works) like a factory with *(many, much) types of cells.
주어가 단수 / 복수명사를 꾸미는 말

→ 우리 몸은 작동한다 / ＿＿＿＿＿＿ / 다양한 종류의 세포를 가진

2 The cells come in (same, different) shapes and sizes
모양과 크기를 꾸미는 말 '다양한'

→ 그 세포들은 나온다(있다) / ＿＿＿＿＿＿ //

and (has, have) different jobs to do.
동사의 주어는 문장 맨 앞의 The cells

→ 그리고 / 가지고 있다 / ＿＿＿＿＿＿ / 해야 할

3 They (form, forms) the parts of our body, such as the skin, heart, (blood, bloody),
주어가 복수 / 나열할 때는 같은 품사끼리

muscles, and bones.

→ 그것들은 구성한다 / ＿＿＿＿＿＿ / 피부, 심장, 혈액, 근육, 뼈와 같은

4 *All these (part, parts) work together to keep the "factory" running (smooth, smoothly).
all + these + 셀 수 있는 명사 복수형 / 원활하게

→ 이 모든 부분이 / ＿＿＿＿＿＿ / "공장"이 원활하게 돌아가도록

5 The human body (create, creates) new cells (grow, to grow) and heal itself.
주어가 단수인 The human body / ~하기 위해서

→ 인체는 생성한다 / ＿＿＿＿＿＿ / 성장하고 스스로 ＿＿＿＿＿＿

6 Cells (make, makes) copies of (itself, themselves).

주어가 복수   재귀대명사: 주어와 일치

→ 세포는 만든다 / ______________

7 Our body replaces (million, millions) of cells (everyday, every day).

million은 셀 수 있는 명사   부사 자리

→ 우리 몸은 교체한다 / ______________ / ______________

8 Over a lifetime, (it, they) produces *(many, a lot of) hair, blood, and (skin, skins).

Our body를 대신   뒤에 셀 수 없는 명사   skin은 셀 수 없는 단수명사

→ ______________ / 그것은 생성한다 / 수많은 머리카락, 혈액, 피부를

9 Our body (need, needs) food, water, and oxygen (to grow, growing) and function.

주어가 단수   to 부정사의 부사적 용법(목적)

→ 우리 몸은 필요로 한다 / ______________ / 성장하고 기능하기 위해

many, a lot of(많은)

many나 a lot of 둘 다 '많은'이란 뜻이지만 many 뒤에는 셀 수 있는 명사의 복수형만, a lot of 뒤에는 셀 수 있는 명사와 셀 수 없는 명사 둘 다 쓸 수 있어요.

- Our body works like a factory with **many** types of cells. (many/a lot of + 셀 수 있는 명사의 복수형)

  (= a lot of) 많은 종류의 세포

- It produces **a lot of** hair, blood, and skin. (a lot of + 셀 수 없는 명사)

  수많은 머리카락, 혈액, 피부를

all(모든)

all은 '모든, 모두의'라는 뜻으로 셀 수 있는 명사와 셀 수 없는 명사 앞에 모두 쓸 수 있어요.

- **All** these parts work together. (all these + 복수명사) 이 모든 부분들
- **All** my money was stolen. (all my + 단수명사) 내 돈 전부

Clothes

A **Speed Reading** 빠르게 읽으며 내용상 중요 단어나 구라고 생각되는 부분에 동그라미 하세요.

Clothes are useful. Humans need clothes to protect their bodies. People wear different clothes to keep warm, stay cool, play sports, or go to school. Clothes can make you look good. Ideas about style and fashion are always changing. They vary from one country to another and throughout human history.

Clothes are made from many different materials. For centuries, all fabrics came from natural things: silk from silkworms, linen and cotton from plants, and wool from sheep. In the late 1800s, people started making artificial fibers. In the 1980s, people began to use natural fibers again.

Words

useful 유용한 ǀ fashion 패션 ǀ vary 다양하다, 달라지다 ǀ throughout ~동안 쭉, 내내 ǀ material 소재 ǀ for centuries 수 세기 동안
fabric 직물, 천 ǀ silkworm 누에 ǀ artificial 인공[인조]의 ǀ fiber 섬유

1   글의 내용과 일치하면 Yes, 틀리면 No에 동그라미 하세요.

1) Clothes can protect the human body.   **Yes**   **No**

2) People can get silk from sheep.   **Yes**   **No**

3) Ideas about fashion are always the same.   **Yes**   **No**

2   글의 내용과 일치하도록 빈칸에 알맞은 단어를 써 보세요. (서술형)

1) A___________ fibers were first made in the late 1800s.
People began using 2) n___________ fibers again in the 1980s.

3   자연으로부터 얻을 수 있는 천 종류 4가지를 영어로 써 보세요. (서술형)

➜

C   **C**hecking Vocabulary   단어를 영어로 바르게 설명한 것을 찾아 연결하세요.

1   artificial   ●   ●   ⓐ   a popular way of dressing during a particular time

2   fiber   ●   ●   ⓑ   not natural; made by humans

3   fabric   ●   ●   ⓒ   a thin thread of something such as wool or cotton

4   fashion   ●   ●   ⓓ   to change, to be different or to become different

5   vary   ●   ●   ⓔ   woven or knitted material, cloth

Reading for Learning

Step **1.** 글의 내용을 생각하며 자세하게 다시 읽기
Step **2.** 빈칸을 채우며 문장 구조 생각하기

1 Clothes are useful. **2** Humans need clothes to protect their bodies. **3** People wear different clothes to keep warm, stay cool, play sports, or go to school. **4** Clothes can make you look good. **5** Ideas about style and fashion are always changing. **6** They vary from one country to another and throughout human history.

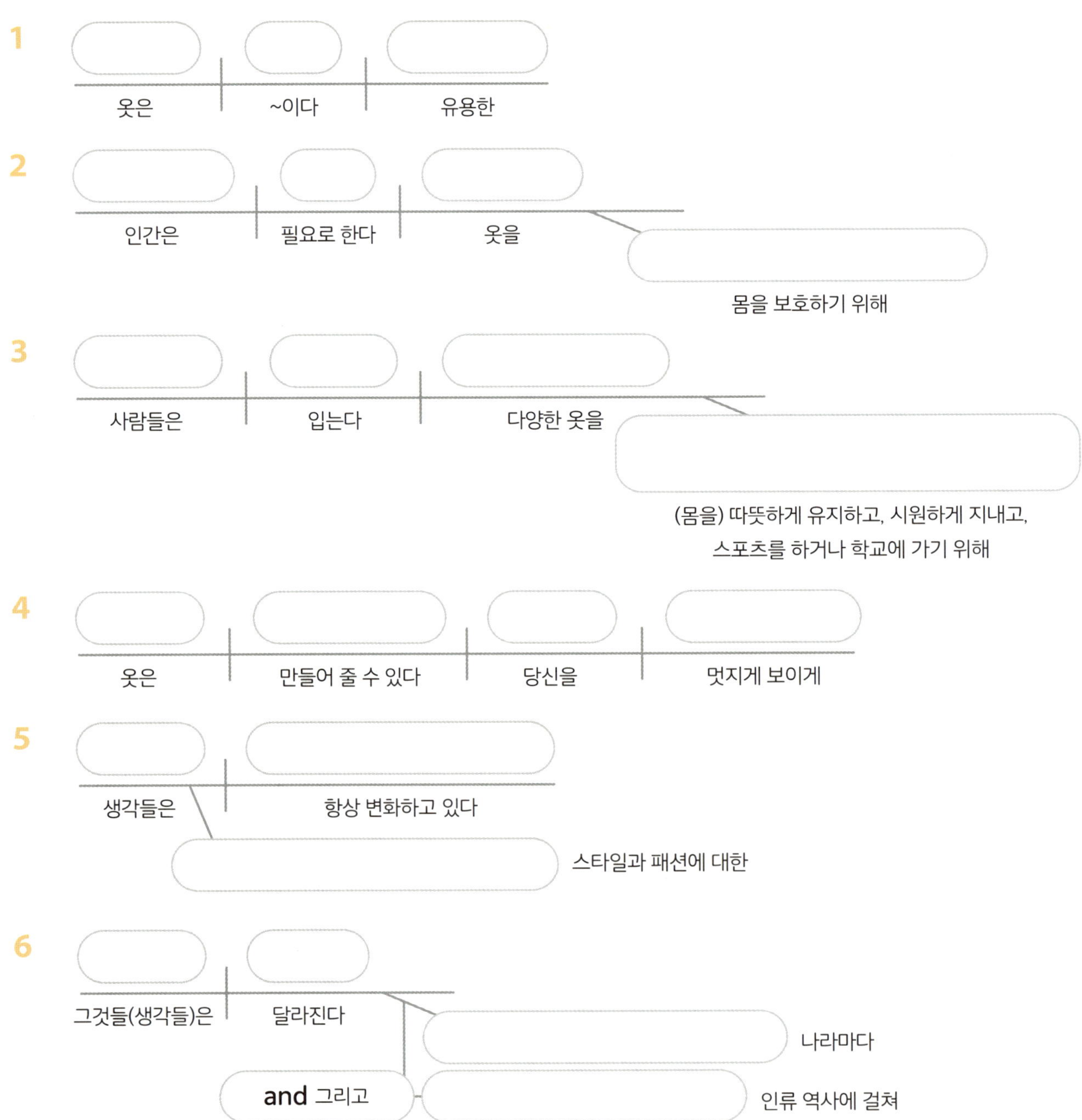

7 Clothes are made from many different materials. **8** For centuries, all fabrics came from natural things: silk from silkworms, linen and cotton from plants, and wool from sheep. **9** In the late 1800s, people started making artificial fibers. **10** In the 1980s, people began to use natural fibers again.

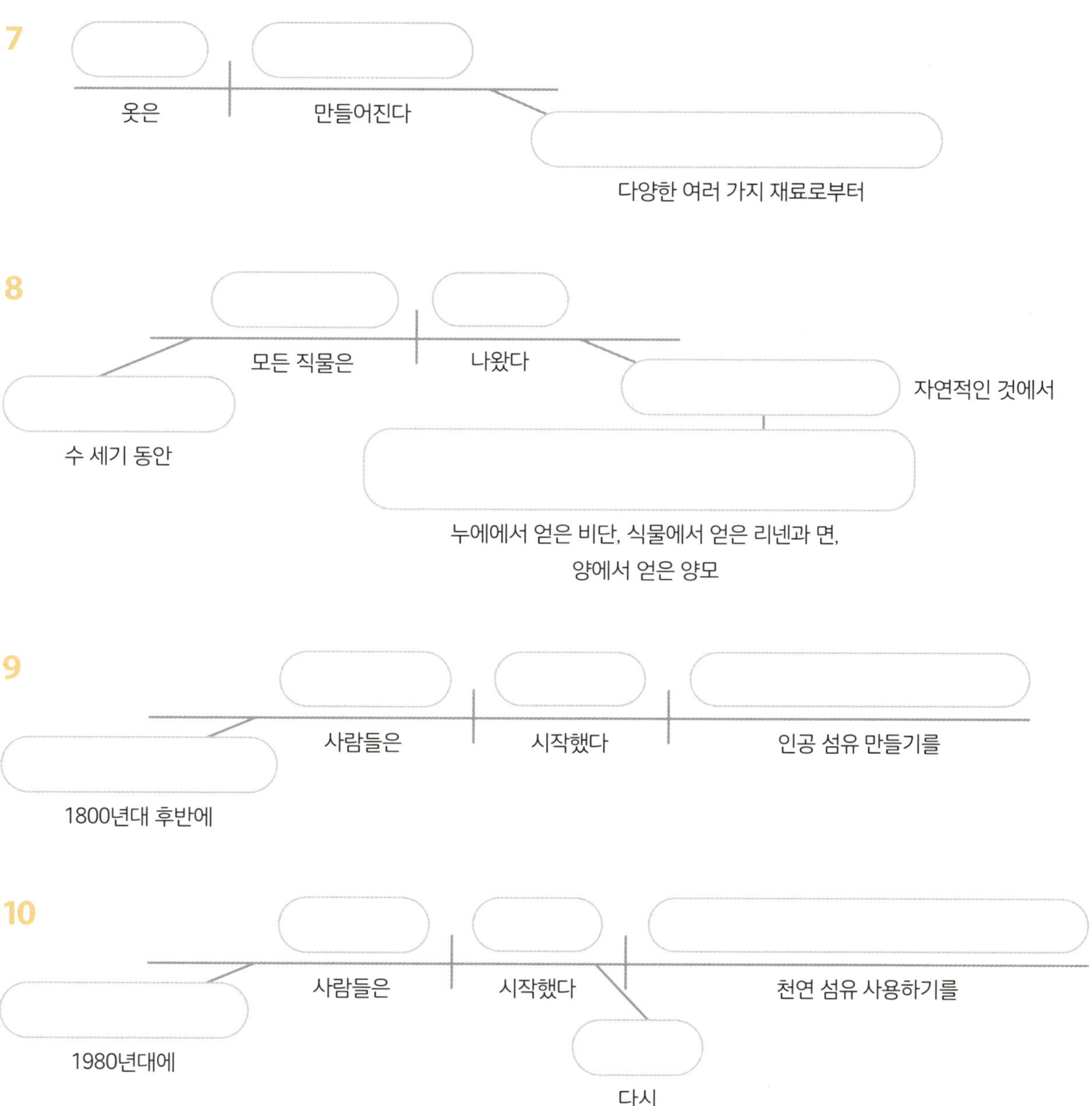

Step **1.** 괄호에서 문장의 흐름에 알맞은 단어나 표현 고르기
Step **2.** 해석에 맞게 끊어 읽기(/) 표시하며 문장을 읽고, 빈칸에 알맞은 해석 쓰기

TIP 읽기 속도를 높이기 위해 짧은 <(접속사 +) 주어 + 동사>는 한 덩어리로 읽기

1 Clothes (is, are) useful.
주어가 복수

→ 옷은 ~이다 / ____________

2 Humans (need, needs) clothes to protect (its, their) bodies.
주어가 복수   복수 humans를 대신하는 인칭대명사

→ 인간은 필요로 한다 / 옷을 / ____________

3 People (wear, wears) different clothes
주어가 복수

→ ____________ / 다양한 옷을 //

to keep warm, stay cool, play sports, or (go, goes) to school.
to부정사의 to가 생략됨

→ 몸을 따뜻하게 유지하고, 시원하게 지내고, 스포츠를 하거나 ____________

4 Clothes can make (your, you) look (good, well).
make + 목적어 + 동사원형   look(~하게 보이다) + 형용사

→ 옷은 만들어 줄 수 있다 / 당신을 / ____________

5 Ideas about style and fashion (is, are) always (change, changing).
Ideas가 주어   진행시제: be + 동사-ing

→ ____________ / 항상 변화하고 있다

6 They (vary, varies) from one country (at, to) another and throughout human history.
주어가 복수   from A to B: A에서 B로

→ 그것(생각)들은 달라진다 / ____________ / 그리고 인류 역사에 걸쳐

7 Clothes are (make, made) from many different (material, materials).

be made from: ~로 만들어지다　　　　　　　　many 뒤에 복수명사

→ ______________________ / 다양한 여러 가지 재료로부터

8 (For, In) centuries, all (fabric, fabrics) came from natural things:

시간 전치사 '~ 동안'　　　all 뒤에 셀 수 있는 명사가 오면 복수형

→ ______________________ / 모든 직물은 나왔다 / 자연적인 것에서 //

silk (from, to) silkworms, linen and cotton from (plant, plants),

~로부터(출처, 기원)　　　　　　　　셀 수 있는 단수명사가 오려면 관사 필요

and wool from (sheep, sheeps).

단수와 복수 형태가 같음

→ ______________________, 식물에서 얻은 리넨과 면, 그리고 양에서 얻은 양모

9 (On, In) the late 1800s, people started *(make, making) artificial fibers.

특정 기간 '동안에'　　　　　　　　start의 목적어로 동명사

→ ______________________ / 사람들은 시작했다 / 인공 섬유 만들기를

10 (On, In) the 1980s, people (begin, began) *to use natural fibers again.

특정 기간 '동안에'　　　　　　　과거에 일어난 일

→ 1980년대에 / 사람들은 시작했다 / ______________________ / 다시

동명사와 to부정사

동명사와 to부정사가 동사 뒤에서 '~하는 것을'이라는 뜻으로 목적어 역할을 해요.

1) 동명사나 to부정사를 목적어로 취하는 동사: **start, begin, like, love**

- People started **making/to make** artificial fibers.

　주어　　동사　　　목적어(인공 섬유 만드는 것을)

- People began **using/to use** natural fibers again.

　주어　　동사　목적어(천연 섬유를 사용하는 것을)

2) 동명사만 목적어로 취하는 동사: **enjoy, finish, keep, mind**

3) to부정사만 목적어로 취하는 동사: **want, hope, decide, plan**

Unit 05 — Deserts

A **Speed Reading** 빠르게 읽으며 내용상 중요 단어나 구라고 생각되는 부분에 동그라미 하세요.

Deserts are the driest places on Earth and receive very little rain. During the day, deserts can be baking hot, but at night they can become freezing cold. Deserts can have sand dunes, rocky hills, or flat plains.

Even though deserts seem empty, many plants and animals live there. Desert plants, like cacti, store water in their thick stems. Camels can go for days without food or water. They store fat in the humps on their backs. People in deserts usually live in tents while traveling. They often stay near oases in search of water.

Words

receive 받다 ∣ baking hot 타는 듯이 더운 ∣ freezing cold 꽁꽁 얼게 추운 ∣ dune 모래 언덕 ∣ rocky 바위로 된 ∣ flat 평평한 ∣ plain 평원
cactus 선인장 (복수형 cacti) ∣ store 저장하다 ∣ stem 줄기 ∣ hump (낙타의) 혹 ∣ travel 여행[이동]하다 ∣ oasis 오아시스 (복수형 oases)
in search of ~을 찾아서

B **R**eading for Information   글을 빠르게 다시 읽고, 아래 질문에 답하세요.

1   글의 내용과 일치하면 Yes, 틀리면 No에 동그라미 하세요.

1) Deserts are wet places.   **Yes**   **No**

2) There are no animals in deserts.   **Yes**   **No**

3) Catci have water in their stems.   **Yes**   **No**

2   글의 내용과 일치하도록 빈칸에 알맞은 단어를 써 보세요. (서술형)

Deserts can be very 1) h___________ or 2) c___________.

There are 3) p___________, animals, and people in the desert.

3   사막에서 볼 수 있는 동물과 식물 이름을 하나씩 우리말로 써 보세요. (서술형)

→ ____

C **C**hecking Vocabulary   단어를 영어로 바르게 설명한 것을 찾아 연결하세요.

1   dune   ●   ●   ⓐ a plant that grows in dry places

2   store   ●   ●   ⓑ a hill of sand near an ocean or in a desert

3   catus   ●   ●   ⓒ to put something away and keep them for future use

4   hump   ●   ●   ⓓ a place in a desert where water and plants are found

5   oasis   ●   ●   ⓔ a lump on the back of an animal (such as a camel)

Step **1.** 글의 내용을 생각하며 자세하게 다시 읽기
Step **2.** 빈칸을 채우며 문장 구조 생각하기

1 Deserts are the driest places on Earth and receive very little rain. **2** During the day, deserts can be baking hot, but at night they can become freezing cold. **3** Deserts can have sand dunes, rocky hills, or flat plains.

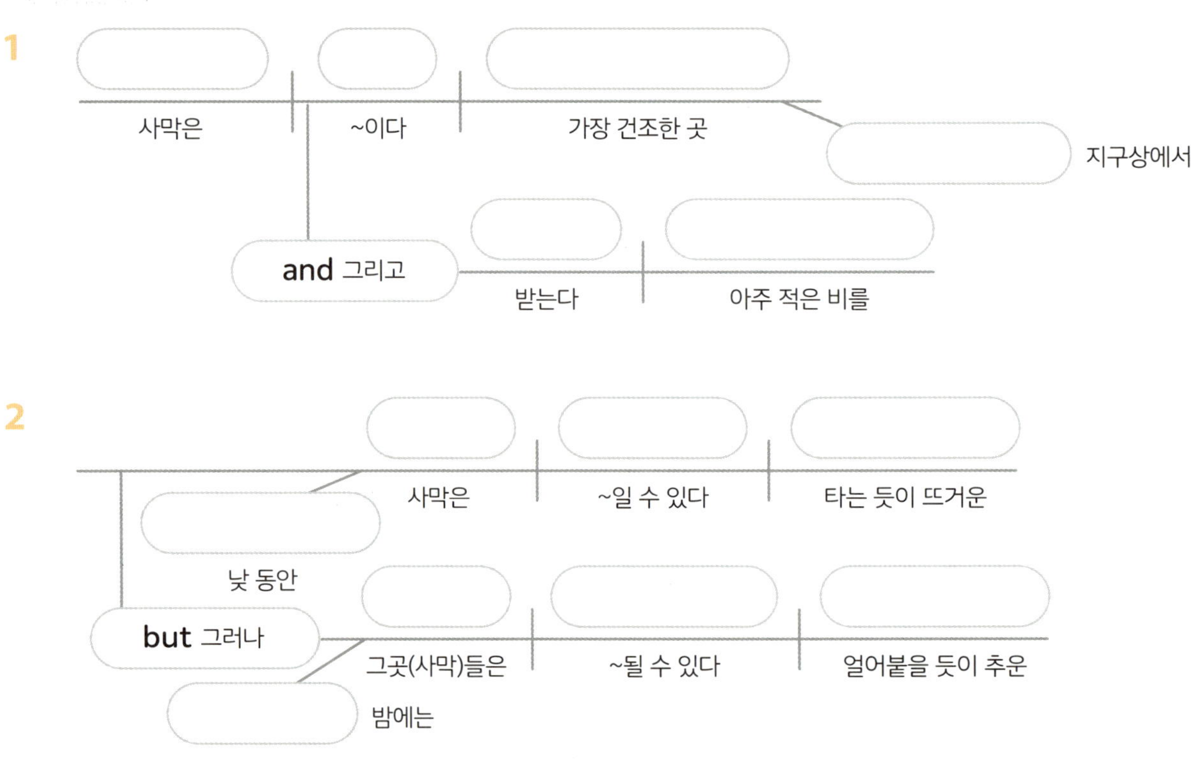

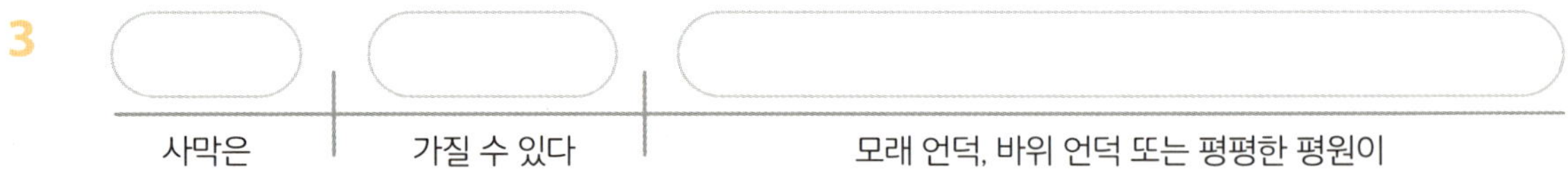

4 Even though deserts seem empty, many plants and animals live there. **5** Desert plants, like cacti, store water in their thick stems. **6** Camels can go for days without food or water. **7** They store fat in the humps on their backs. **8** People in deserts usually live in tents while traveling. **9** They often stay near oases in search of water.

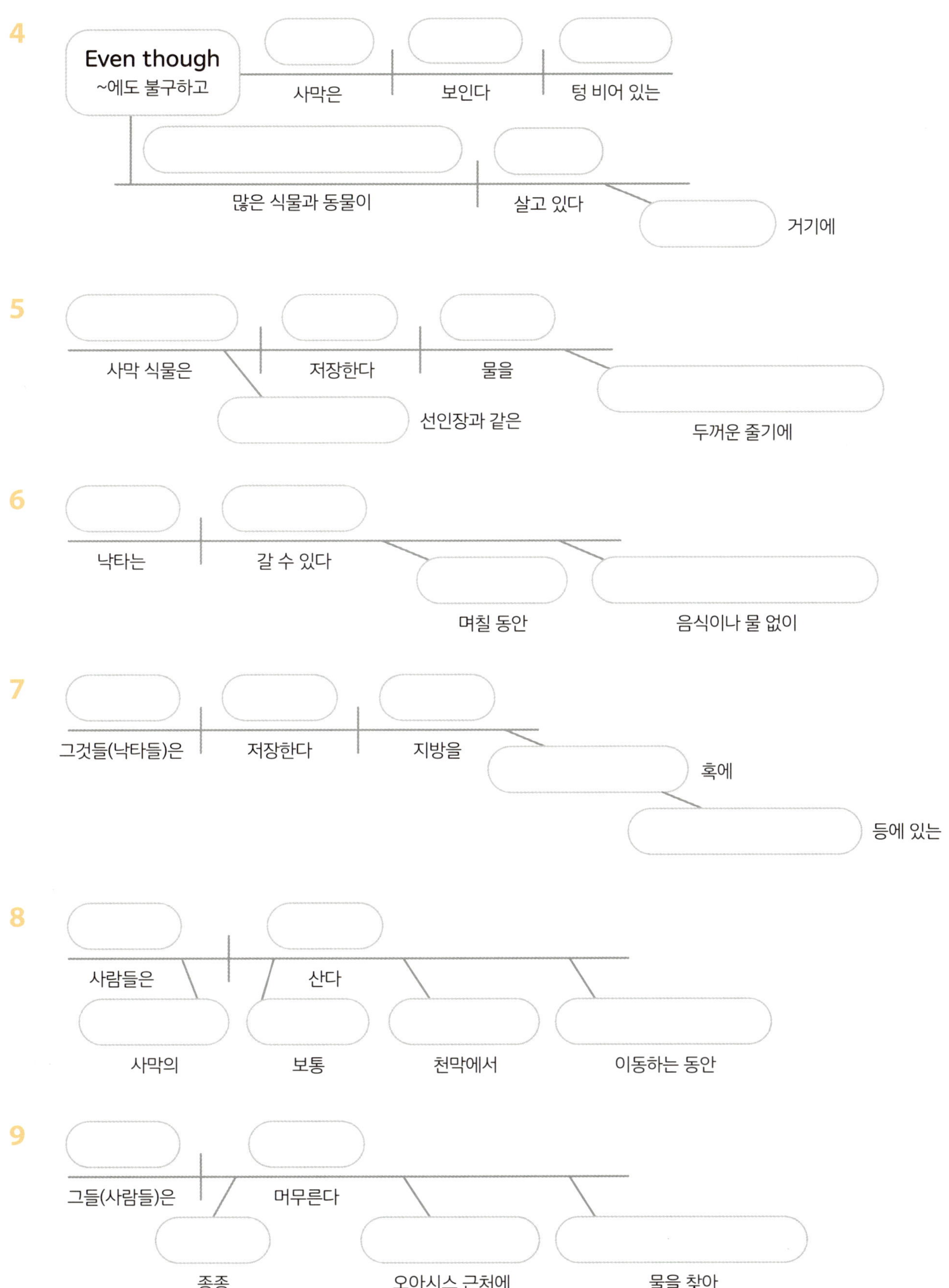
4
Even though
~에도 불구하고
사막은
보인다
텅 비어 있는
많은 식물과 동물이
살고 있다
거기에

5
사막 식물은
저장한다
물을
선인장과 같은
두꺼운 줄기에

6
낙타는
갈 수 있다
며칠 동안
음식이나 물 없이

7
그것들(낙타들)은
저장한다
지방을
혹에
등에 있는

8
사람들은
산다
사막의
보통
천막에서
이동하는 동안

9
그들(사람들)은
머무른다
종종
오아시스 근처에
물을 찾아

Step **1.** 괄호에서 문장의 흐름에 알맞은 단어나 표현 고르기
Step **2.** 해석에 맞게 끊어 읽기(/) 표시하며 문장을 읽고, 빈칸에 알맞은 해석 쓰기

TIP 읽기 속도를 높이기 위해 짧은 <(접속사 +) 주어 + 동사>는 한 덩어리로 읽기

1 Deserts (is, are) the driest places on Earth and receive very *(few, little) rain.
　　　　주어가 복수　　　　　　　　　　　　　　　　　　뒤에 오는 rain은 셀 수 없는 명사

→ 사막은 ~이다 / 지구상에서 ＿＿＿＿＿＿＿＿＿＿ / 그리고 받지 (않는다) / 비를 거의

2 (During, At) the day, deserts can (is, be) baking hot,
　　　　~ 동안　　　　　　　　　　조동사 + 동사원형

→ ＿＿＿＿＿＿＿＿ / 사막은 ~일 수 있다 / 타는 듯이 뜨거운 //

but (on, at) night (it, they) can become freezing cold.
　　　　~에(시간)　　주어 deserts를 대신하는 말

→ 그러나 밤에 / 사막은 ~될 수 있다 / ＿＿＿＿＿＿＿＿＿＿

3 (Desserts, Deserts) can (has, have) sand dunes, (rock, rocky) hills, or flat plains.
　　　　후식 vs 사막　　　　　　조동사 + 동사원형　　　　　명사를 꾸며주는 형용사

→ 사막에는 있을 수 있다 / 모래 언덕, ＿＿＿＿＿＿＿ 또는 평평한 평원이

4 *Even though deserts (seem, seems) empty,
　　　　　　　　　　주어가 복수

→ 사막이 ~처럼 보일지라도 / ＿＿＿＿＿＿＿ //

(many, much) plants and animals live there.
복수명사 앞에서 쓸 수 있는 것

→ 많은 ＿＿＿＿＿＿＿＿＿ 산다 / 거기에

5 Desert plants, like cacti, (store, stores) (a water, water) in their thick stems.
　　　　　　　　　　　　plants가 주어　　water는 셀 수 없는 명사

→ 선인장과 같은 사막 식물은 / ＿＿＿＿＿＿＿ / ＿＿＿＿＿＿＿ / 그것들의 두꺼운 줄기에

6 Camels can (goes, go) for days (with, without) (a food, food) or water.

　　조동사 + 동사원형　　　　　　　　　~없이　　　food는 셀 수 없는 명사

➜ 낙타는 갈 수 있다 / 며칠 동안 / ___________

7 They (store, stores) fat in the humps (in, on) their backs.

　　주어가 복수　　　　　　　　　　~ 위에(접촉)

➜ 그것들은(낙타는) 저장한다 / ___________ / 혹에 / 등에 있는

8 People (under, in) deserts (usually live, live usually) in tents while traveling.

　　(공간 내의) ~에서　　　　　　빈도부사 위치는 일반동사 앞

➜ 사막에 있는 사람들은 / 보통 산다 / ___________ / 이동하는 동안

9 They (stay often, often stay) near oases in search of water.

　　빈도부사 위치는 일반동사 앞

➜ 그들은 종종 머무른다 / ___________ / 물을 찾아서

수량 형용사 little

'거의 없는'이라는 뜻으로 셀 수 없는 명사와 함께 써요.

- Deserts are the driest places on Earth and receive very **little** rain.

　　　　　　　　　　　비가 거의 내리지 않는다

cf) 같은 의미의 few는 그 뒤에 셀 수 있는 명사의 복수형과 함께 써요.

　　She has **few words**. 말수가 적다

접속사 even though

'비록 ~일지라도', '~에도 불구하고'라는 의미로 두 문장을 이어주는 접속사예요.

- Deserts seem empty. + Many plants and animals live there.

　→ **Even though** deserts seem empty, many plants and animals live there.

　　사막이 텅 비어 보일지라도, 많은 식물과 동물이 그곳에 살고 있다.

Unit 06 — Eating

A · Speed Reading · 빠르게 읽으며 내용상 중요 단어나 구라고 생각되는 부분에 동그라미 하세요.

Food gives you energy. It helps you grow and keeps you healthy. Your body lets you know that it needs food by making you feel hungry. When you eat, you chew and swallow the food. This allows your body to collect nutrients from the food. The leftovers then travel through your digestive system.

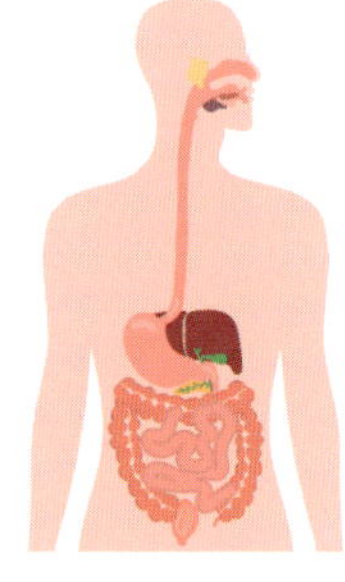

Digestion begins in the mouth. As you chew, food mixes with a liquid called saliva. It starts breaking down food into a watery mush. Special cells in your digestive system then absorb the nutrients. Finally, the smelly leftovers, along with billions of dead bacteria, are ready to exit the body.

Words

healthy 건강한 | chew 씹다 | swallow 삼키다 | allow 허락하다, 가능하게 하다 | nutrient 영양소 | leftover 나머지, 남은 음식
digestive 소화의 (digestion 소화) | saliva 침, 타액 | break down ~을 부수다 | watery 물기가 많은 | mush 곤죽 (같은 덩어리)
absorb 흡수하다 | smelly 냄새 나는 | billion 10억 | bacteria 박테리아, 세균 | exit 나가다

   Reading for Information   글을 빠르게 다시 읽고, 아래 질문에 답하세요.

1   글의 내용과 일치하면 Yes, 틀리면 No에 동그라미 하세요.

1) You get energy from food.   **Yes**   **No**

2) Food mixes with nutrients.   **Yes**   **No**

3) Your body collects nutrients.   **Yes**   **No**

2   글의 내용과 일치하도록 빈칸에 알맞은 단어를 써 보세요. (서술형)

Digestion starts in the 1) m____________, when you eat food.
During the 2) d____________, your body collects the 3) n____________ from the food.

3   몸에 음식이 필요한 것을 어떻게 알게 되는지 우리말로 써 보세요. (서술형)

→ ～～～～～～～～～～～～～～～～～～～～～～～～～～～～～～～～～～～～～～～

C   **Checking Vocabulary**   단어를 영어로 바르게 설명한 것을 찾아 연결하세요.

1   energy   ●   ●   ⓐ   to get out of or leave something

2   chew   ●   ●   ⓑ   the ability to do work or cause change

3   nutrient   ●   ●   ⓒ   to take in liquid, gas, or heat and hold it

4   absorb   ●   ●   ⓓ   to break food into small pieces with your teeth

5   exit   ●   ●   ⓔ   something in food that helps people, animals, and
plants live and grow

Step **1.** 글의 내용을 생각하며 자세하게 다시 읽기
Step **2.** 빈칸을 채우며 문장 구조 생각하기

1 Food gives you energy. **2** It helps you grow and keeps you healthy. **3** Your body lets you know that it needs food by making you feel hungry. **4** When you eat, you chew and swallow the food. **5** This allows your body to collect nutrients from the food. **6** The leftovers then travel through your digestive system.

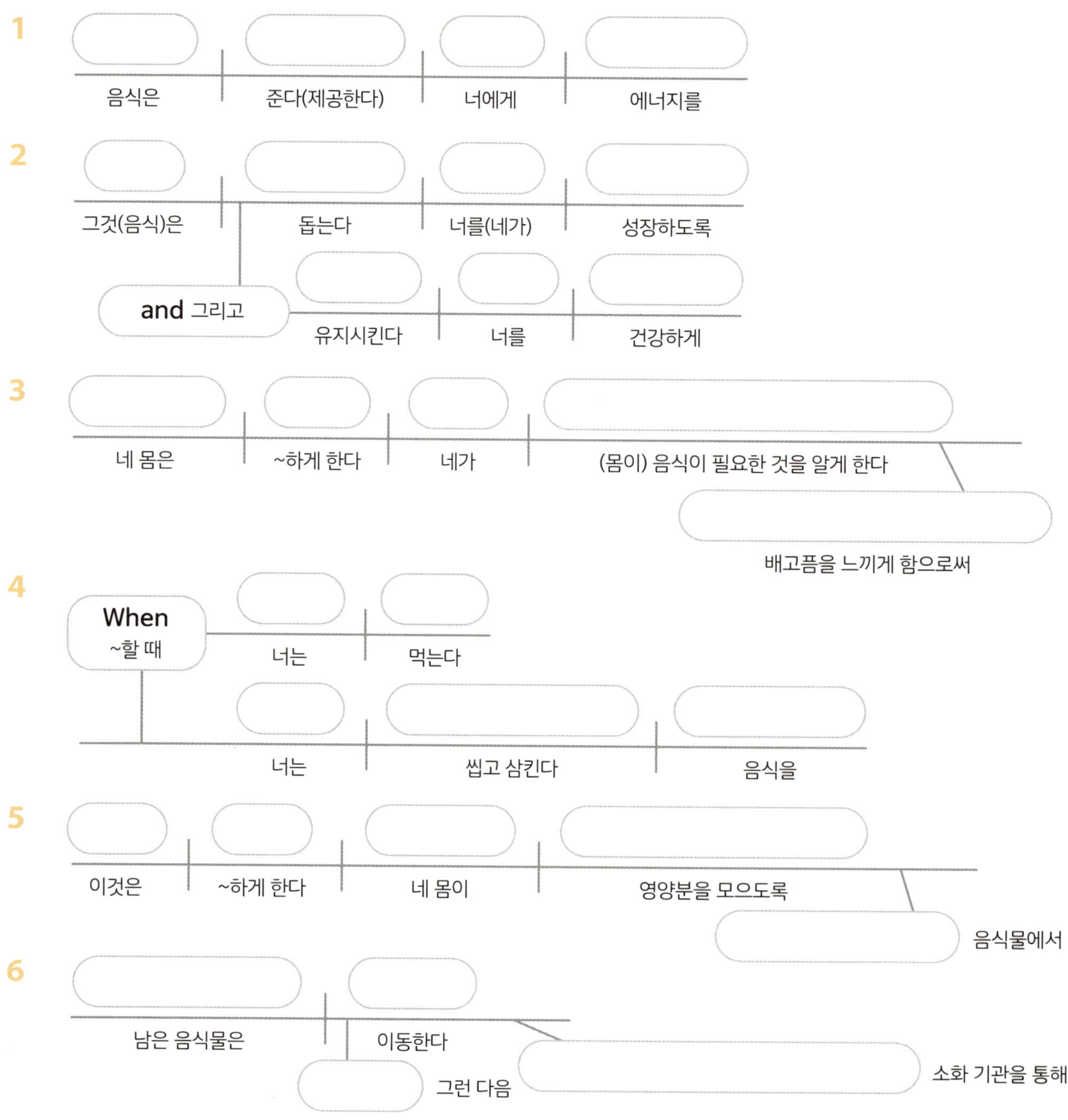

7 Digestion begins in the mouth. **8** As you chew, food mixes with a liquid called saliva. **9** It starts breaking down food into a watery mush. **10** Special cells in your digestive system then absorb the nutrients. **11** Finally, the smelly leftovers, along with billions of dead bacteria, are ready to exit the body.

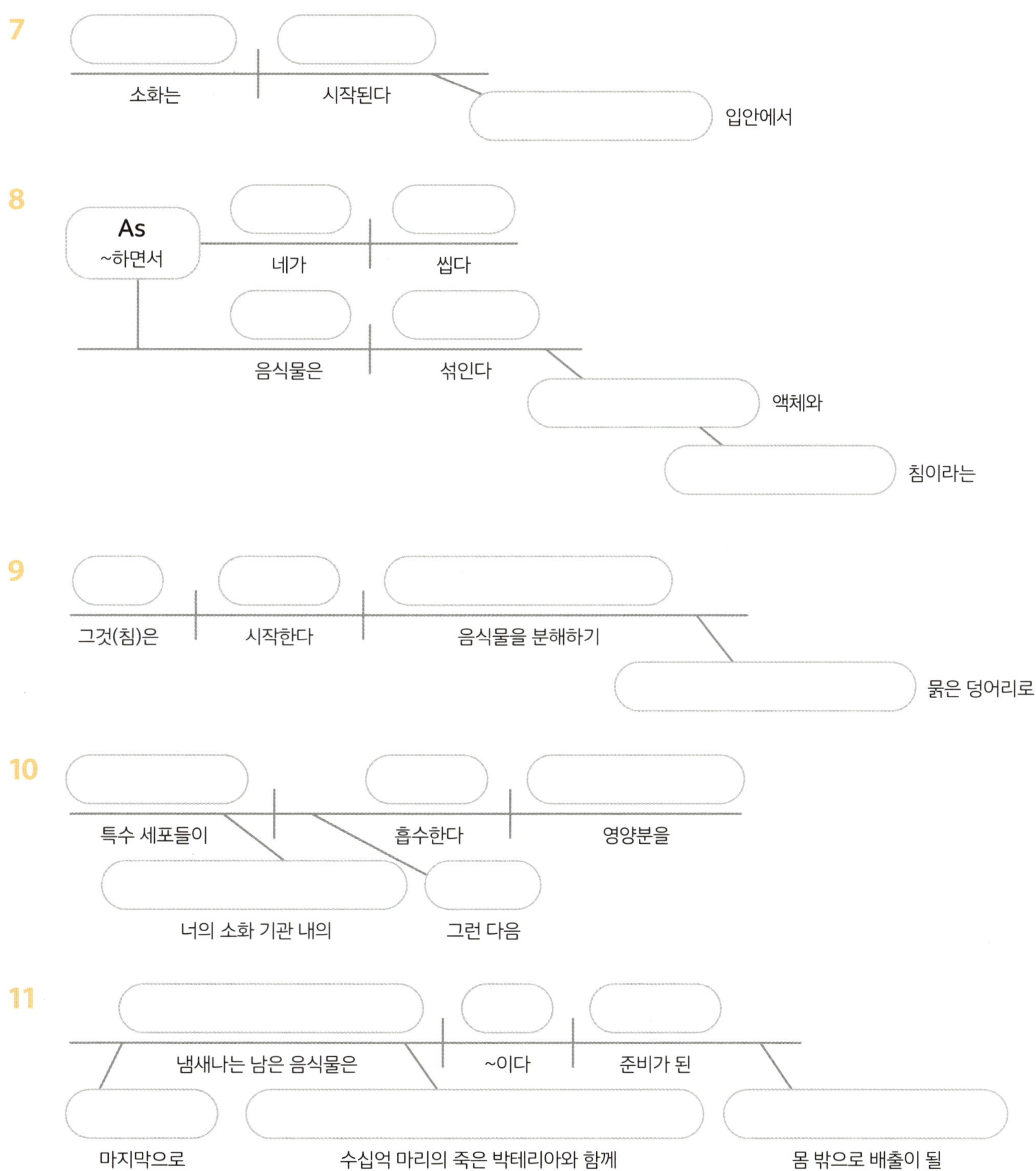

E   Grammar for Reading

Step **1.** 괄호에서 문장의 흐름에 알맞은 단어나 표현 고르기

Step **2.** 해석에 맞게 끊어 읽기(/) 표시하며 문장을 읽고, 빈칸에 알맞은 해석 쓰기

TIP 읽기 속도를 높이기 위해 짧은 <(접속사 +) 주어 + 동사>는 한 덩어리로 읽기

1   Food *(give, gives) you (energy, an energy).
　　　단수 주어　　　　　　energy는 셀 수 없는 명사

→ 음식은 제공한다 / 너에게 / ＿＿＿＿＿＿＿

2   It *helps (your, you) grow and keeps you (health, healthy).
　　　help + 목적어 + 목적 보어　　　　　keep + 형용사: ~한 상태를 유지하다

→ 그것(음식)은 돕는다 / ＿＿＿＿＿＿＿ / 그리고 유지해 준다 / 너를 건강하게

3   Your body *lets you (to know, know) that it needs food by (make, making) you feel hungry.
　　　let + 목적어 + 목적 보어(동사원형)　　　　전치사 by + 동명사

→ 네 몸은 ~하게 한다 / 네가 / 그것(몸)이 음식이 필요하다는 것을 알게 한다 / ＿＿＿＿＿＿＿

4   (When, After) you eat, you chew and (swallow, to swallow) the food.
　　　~할 때　　　　　　　　　and는 앞뒤 같은 품사 연결

→ 네가 음식을 먹을 때 / 너는 ＿＿＿＿＿＿＿ / 음식을

5   This (allow, allows) your body (to collect, collect) nutrients from the food.
　　　주어가 단수　　　　allow + 목적어 + 목적 보어(to do)

→ 이것은 ~하게 한다 / 네 몸이 / ＿＿＿＿＿＿＿ / 음식물에서

6   The leftovers then (travel, travels) through your digestive system.
　　　　　주어가 복수

→ 남은 음식물은 / 그런 다음 이동한다 / ＿＿＿＿＿＿＿

7   Digestion begins (in, on) the mouth.
　　　　(공간) 안에서

→ 소화는 시작된다 / ＿＿＿＿＿＿＿

8   As you chew, (a food, food) mixes with a liquid (called, call) saliva.

food는 셀 수 없는 명사 · 불리는

➜ 네가 씹을 때 / 음식물은 섞인다 / _____________ / 침이라는

9   (It, They) starts breaking down food into a (watery, water) mush.

saliva를 대신하는 대명사 · a + 형용사 + 명사

➜ 그것(침)은 시작한다 / _____________ / 묽은 덩어리로

10   Special cells in your digestive system then (absorb, absorbs) the nutrients.

주어는 cells

➜ 특수 세포들이 / _____________ / 그런 다음 흡수한다 / 영양분을

11   (Final, Finally), the smelly leftovers, along with billions of dead bacteria,

마침내, 마지막으로

➜ 마지막으로 / _____________ / 수십억 마리의 죽은 박테리아와 함께 //

(is, are) ready (exit, to exit) the body.

주어는 leftovers · be ready to + 동사원형

➜ ~이다 / 준비가 된 / _____________

Grammar Point

수여동사 + 간접 목적어(~에게) + 직접 목적어(…을/를)

give(주다), **send**(보내다), **show**(보여주다), **tell**(말해주다)

주는 행동을 나타내는 동사인 수여동사 뒤에는 목적어를 2개 써요. 해석은 '~에게 …을/를 주다[보내다, 보여주다, 말해주다]'라고 해요.

- Food **gives you energy**. (너에게 에너지를 주다)

사역동사 + 목적어(~가) + 목적 보어(…하게)

help(돕다), **let**(~하게 허락하다), **have**(~하게 하다), **make**(강제로 ~하게 하다)

남에게 하게 하는 동사인 사역동사 뒤에는 목적 보어로 동사원형을 써요. 목적어와 목적 보어를 주어와 동사처럼 해석해요.

- It **helps you grow**. (네가 성장하게 돕다)
- Your body **lets you know**. (네가 알게 하다)

Unit 07

Family

A **Speed Reading** 빠르게 읽으며 내용상 중요 단어나 구라고 생각되는 부분에 동그라미 하세요.

The people you live with are your family. Families engage in various activities together. They eat, play, talk, and do chores together. Families come in all shapes and sizes. Some are large, while others are small, with just one parent and one or two children. Even pets can be part of a family.

Your body functions and grows based on instructions called genes, which are found in all your cells. These genes are inherited from your biological parents — half coming from your mother and half from your father. Identical twins look exactly alike because they share the same genes.

Words

engage in ~에 참여하다 | various 다양한 | chores 허드렛일 | even ~도[조차], 심지어 | based on ~에 근거하여 | instruction 설명, 지시
gene 유전자 | inherit 상속하다, 물려받다 | biological 생물체의, 생물학의 | identical twins 일란성 쌍생아 (identical 동일한)
exactly 정확히 | alike 서로 같은, 꼭 닮은

B **R**eading for Information 글을 빠르게 다시 읽고, 아래 질문에 답하세요.

1 글의 내용과 일치하면 Yes, 틀리면 No에 동그라미 하세요.

1) Families all look the same.   **Yes**   **No**

2) The people you live with are your family.   **Yes**   **No**

3) All genes come from your mother.   **Yes**   **No**

2 글의 내용과 일치하도록 빈칸에 공통으로 들어갈 단어를 써 보세요. (서술형)

- Your body works and grows using instructions called ___________.

- Your ___________ are passed on to you by your biological parents.

3 일란성 쌍둥이가 똑같아 보이는 이유를 우리말로 써 보세요. (서술형)

→ ____

C **C**hecking Vocabulary 단어를 영어로 바르게 설명한 것을 찾아 연결하세요.

1 chores •   • ⓐ the part of a cell which controls its physical characteristics, growth, and development

2 gene •   • ⓑ exactly the same

3 biological •   • ⓒ tasks such as cleaning, washing, and ironing that somebody must do at home

4 identical •   • ⓓ something that someone tells you to do

5 instruction •   • ⓔ used to describe processes and states that occur in the bodies and cells of living things

Step **1.** 글의 내용을 생각하며 자세하게 다시 읽기
Step **2.** 빈칸을 채우며 문장 구조 생각하기

1 The people you live with are your family. **2** Families engage in various activities together. **3** They eat, play, talk, and do chores together. **4** Families come in all shapes and sizes. **5** Some are large, while others are small, with just one parent and one or two children. **6** Even pets can be part of a family.

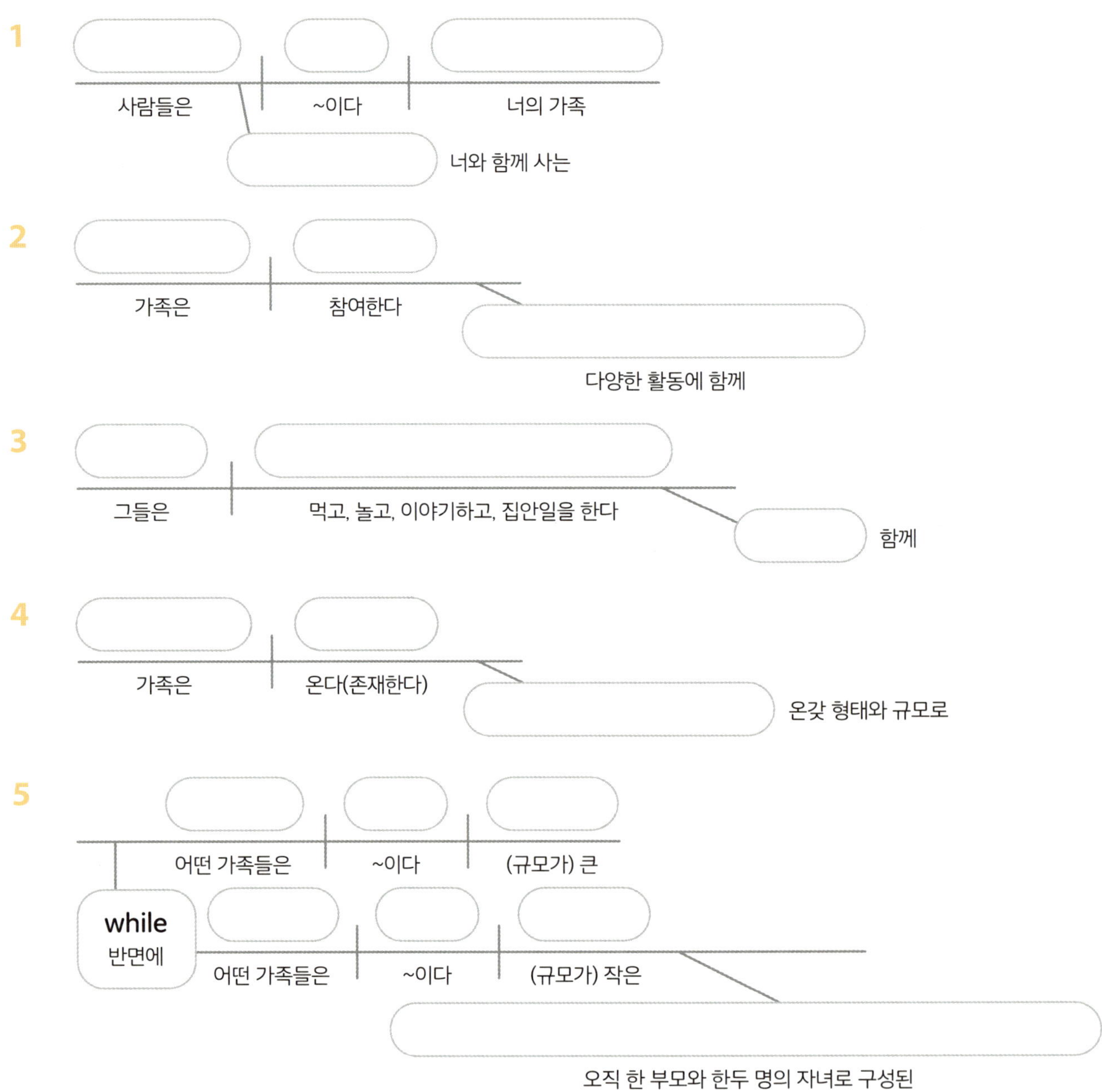

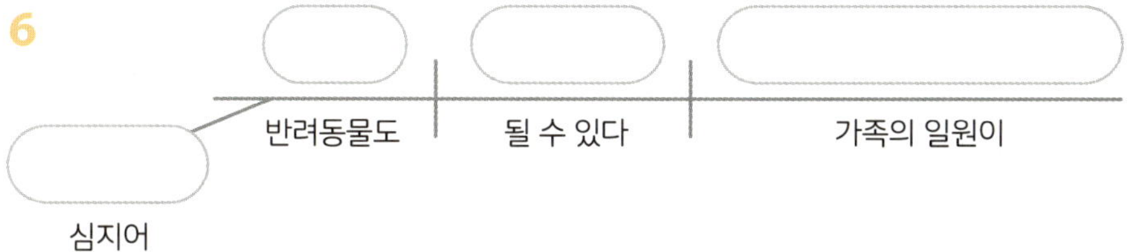

6

심지어 | 반려동물도 | 될 수 있다 | 가족의 일원이

---

7 Your body functions and grows based on instructions called genes, which are found in all your cells. **8** These genes are inherited from your biological parents — half coming from your mother and half from your father. **9** Identical twins look exactly alike because they share the same genes.

7

네 몸은 | 기능하고 성장한다

유전자라 불리는 명령에 따라

모든 세포에서 발견되는

8

이 유전자는 | 물려받는다

친부모로부터

절반은 어머니에게서

and ~와

절반은 아버지에게서

9

일란성 쌍둥이는 | 보인다 | 완전히 똑같은

because
왜냐하면

그들(일란성 쌍둥이)은 | 공유한다 | 같은 유전자를

E Grammar for Reading

Step **1.** 괄호에서 문장의 흐름에 알맞은 단어나 표현 고르기
Step **2.** 해석에 맞게 끊어 읽기(/) 표시하며 문장을 읽고, 빈칸에 알맞은 해석 쓰기

TIP 읽기 속도를 높이기 위해 짧은 <(접속사 +) 주어 + 동사>는 한 덩어리로 읽기

1 *The people you live with (is, are) your family.
주어가 복수

→ 사람들은 / ________________ / ~이다 / 너의 가족

2 Families (engage, engages) in various activities together.
주어가 복수

→ 가족은 참여한다 / ________________ / 함께

3 *They (eat, eats), play, talk, and (do, to do) chores together.
주어가 복수   and는 앞 품사와 같은 것 연결

→ 그들은 먹고, / 놀고, 이야기하고, ________________ 한다 / 함께

4 Families (come, comes) in all (a shape, shapes) and sizes.
주어가 복수   all + 복수명사

→ 가족은 존재한다 / 온갖 ________________

5 Some (is, are) large,
주어 Some은 복수

→ 어떤 가족들은 ~이다 / 큰(대가족) //

while (other, others) are small, with just one (parent, parents) and one or two (child, children).
other는 단수 또는 형용사   아버지나 어머니 한 사람   two + 복수명사

→ 반면에 어떤 가족들은 ~이다 / 작은(소가족), / ________________ 한두 명 자녀로만 구성된

6 Even pets can (be, is) part of a family.
조동사 + 동사원형

→ 심지어 반려동물도 / ~될 수 있다 / ________________

7　*Your body (function, functions) and (grow, grows) based on instructions called genes,
body가 주어　　　　　　　　body가 주어

➜ 너의 몸은 / 작동하고 성장한다 / ＿＿＿＿＿＿ / 유전자라 불리는 //

which are found in all your (cell, cells).
all + 소유격 + 복수명사

➜ (그것은) 발견된다 / 너의 ＿＿＿＿＿＿ 안에서

8　*These genes (is, are) inherited (to, from) your biological (parent, parents)
주어가 복수　　　　　　　~로부터　　　　　　　아버지와 어머니 둘다

➜ 이 유전자들은 물려받는다 / ＿＿＿＿＿＿ //

— half coming (to, from) your mother (and, or) half from your father.
~로부터　　　　　　　그리고

➜ 절반은 어머니에게서 오고 / 그리고 ＿＿＿＿＿＿

9　Identical twins (look, looks) exactly (alike, different).
주어가 복수

➜ 일란성 쌍둥이는 ~하게 보인다 / ＿＿＿＿＿＿ //

because (it, they) share the (same, different) genes.
twins를 대신

➜ 그들이 공유하기 때문에 / ＿＿＿＿＿＿

문장의 주어와 동사 수 일치

문장의 동사는 주어가 단수 또는 복수인지 먼저 확인 후 이에 맞춰서 형태를 결정해야 해요.

- **The people** you live with are your family. (복수 주어 - 복수 be동사)
- **They** eat, play, talk, and do chores together. (복수 주어 - 일반동사의 원형)
- **Your body** functions and grows based on instructions called genes. (단수 주어 - 3인칭 단수동사)
- **These genes** are inherited from your biological parents. (복수 주어 - 복수 be동사)

Unit 08

Feelings

A **Speed Reading** 빠르게 읽으며 내용상 중요 단어나 구라고 생각되는 부분에 동그라미 하세요.

We can have many feelings. We might feel happy or sad, excited or bored. Sometimes we can feel calm or angry. We show our feelings in different ways. For example, when we laugh, it shows others that we are having fun. Sometimes we cry even when we feel very happy.

Everyone has feelings, but people don't feel the same way. Some people love spending time alone, while others feel lonely even after a short time alone. Some people like spiders, while others are afraid of them. Some people enjoy watching scary movies or taking roller coaster rides because they like the thrill of feeling scared!

Words

might ~할지도 모른다 ㅣ excited 흥분한 ㅣ bored 지루한 ㅣ calm 침착한 ㅣ for example 예를 들어
scary 무서운, 무섭게 하는 (scared 무서워하는, 겁먹은) ㅣ roller coaster 롤러코스터 ㅣ ride 놀이기구, 타기 ㅣ thrill 흥분, 전율

Reading for Information 글을 빠르게 다시 읽고, 아래 질문에 답하세요.

1 글의 내용과 일치하면 Yes, 틀리면 No에 동그라미 하세요.

1) We cannot show many feelings.　　**Yes**　**No**

2) We cry even when we feel happy.　　**Yes**　**No**

3) Everyone feels the same way.　　**Yes**　**No**

2 글의 내용과 일치하도록 빈칸에 공통으로 들어갈 단어를 써 보세요. (서술형)

- We can have many ___________.
- Everyone has ___________ but they don't feel the same way.

3 사람들이 무서운 영화를 보는 것이나 롤러코스터 타기를 좋아하는 이유를 우리말로 써 보세요. (서술형)

➜ ____

C **Checking Vocabulary** 단어를 영어로 바르게 설명한 것을 찾아 연결하세요.

1 calm ● ● ⓐ an emotion, such as anger or happiness

2 feeling ● ● ⓑ causing fear; frightening

3 scary ● ● ⓒ strong feeling of excitement or pleasure

4 thrill ● ● ⓓ not excited or not angry

5 roller coaster ● ● ⓔ an amusement park ride in which a train of open cars rides up and down a winding track

Reading for Learning

Step **1.** 글의 내용을 생각하며 자세하게 다시 읽기
Step **2.** 빈칸을 채우며 문장 구조 생각하기

1 We can have many feelings. **2** We might feel happy or sad, excited or bored. **3** Sometimes we can feel calm or angry. **4** We show our feelings in different ways. **5** For example, when we laugh, it shows others that we are having fun. **6** Sometimes we cry even when we feel very happy.

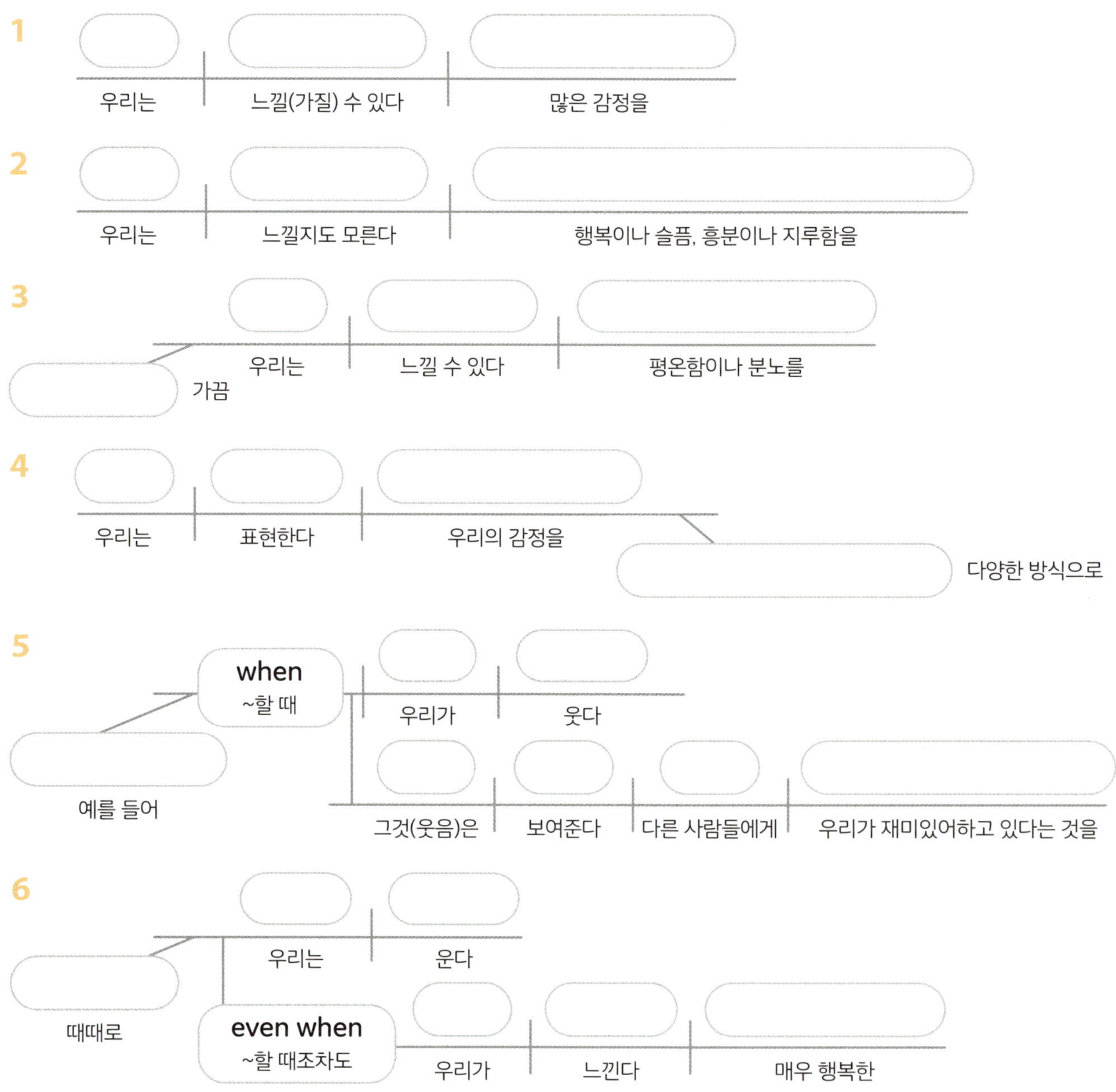

7 Everyone has feelings, but people don't feel the same way. 8 Some people love spending time alone, while others feel lonely even after a short time alone. 9 Some people like spiders, while others are afraid of them. 10 Some people enjoy watching scary movies or taking roller coaster rides because they like the thrill of feeling scared!

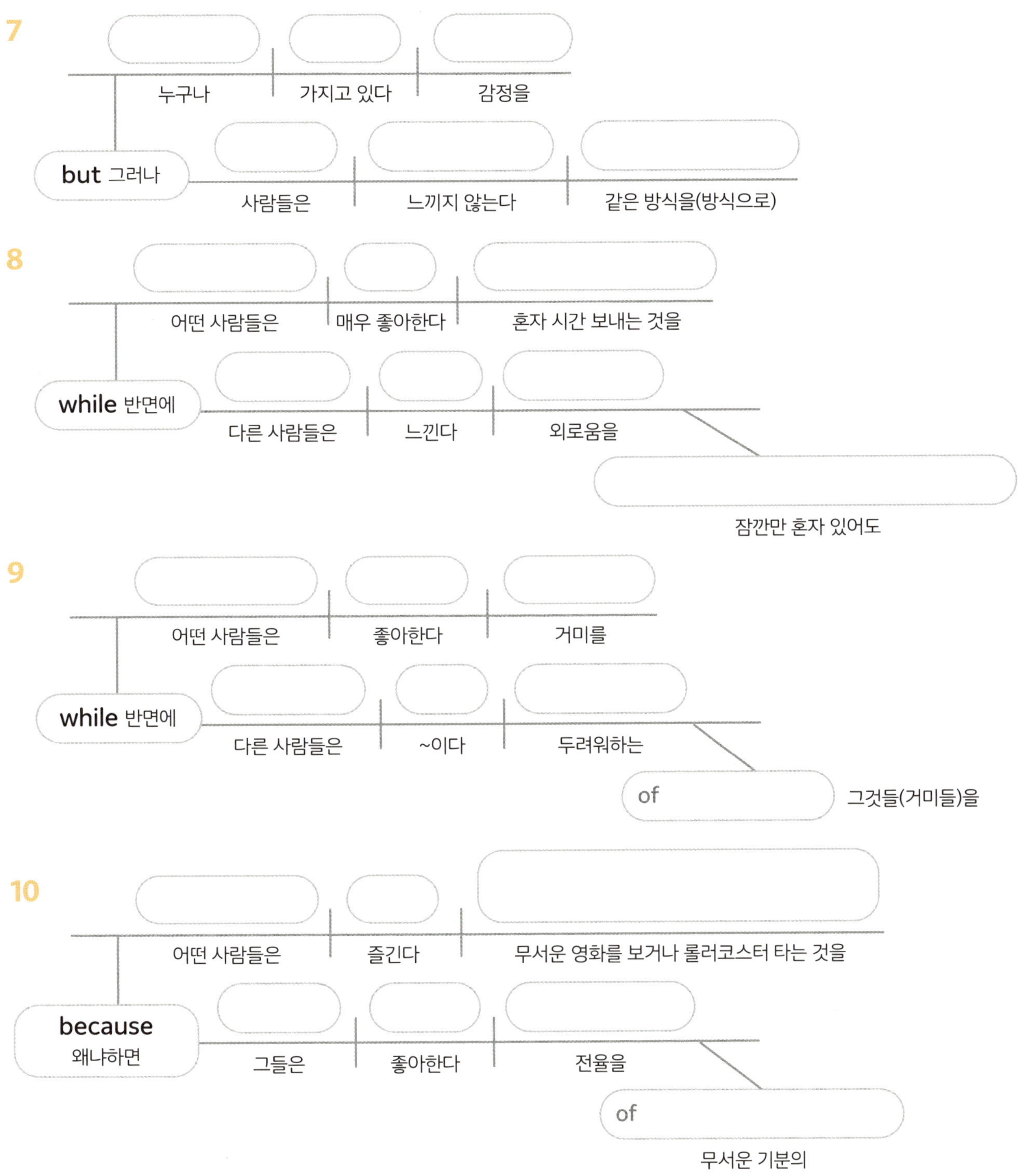

Grammar for Reading

Step **1.** 괄호에서 문장의 흐름에 알맞은 단어나 표현 고르기
Step **2.** 해석에 맞게 끊어 읽기(/) 표시하며 문장을 읽고, 빈칸에 알맞은 해석 쓰기

🔊 *TIP* 읽기 속도를 높이기 위해 짧은 <(접속사 +) 주어 + 동사>는 한 덩어리로 읽기

1 We can have (much, many) feelings.
복수명사를 꾸미는 것

➜ 우리는 가질 수 있다 / ＿＿＿＿＿＿＿＿＿

2 We might feel happy or (sad, sadly), excited *or (bored, boring).
feel + 형용사   지루한 vs 지루하게 하는

➜ ＿＿＿＿＿＿＿＿＿＿ / 행복이나 슬픔, 흥분이나 지루함을

3 Sometimes we can feel (calm, calmly) or angry.
feel + 형용사

➜ 가끔 / ＿＿＿＿＿＿＿＿＿ / 평온함이나 분노를

4 We show (us, our) feelings in different ways.
인칭대명사 소유격 + 명사

➜ 우리는 표현한다 / ＿＿＿＿＿＿＿ / 다양한 방식으로

5 (For, at) example, when we laugh,

➜ ＿＿＿＿＿＿ / 우리가 웃을 때 //

it (show, shows) others that we are (have, having) fun.
주어가 단수   be동사 + 동사-ing: ~하고 있다

➜ 그것(웃음)은 보여준다 / 다른 사람들에게 / ＿＿＿＿＿＿＿＿＿＿

6 Sometimes we cry even when we feel very (happy, happily).
동사 feel의 보어

➜ 때때로 / ＿＿＿＿＿＿＿ / 우리가 ~라고 느낄 때 조차도 / 매우 행복한

7 Everyone (have, has) feelings, but people (doesn't, don't) feel the same way.

    everyone은 단수 취급   복수 주어

➜ 누구나 가지고 있다 / 감정을 / 그러나 사람들은 느끼지 않는다 / ﹏﹏﹏﹏﹏

8 Some (person, people) love (spending, spend) time alone,

    some + 복수명사   love의 목적어

➜ 어떤 사람들은 매우 좋아한다 / ﹏﹏﹏﹏﹏﹏﹏﹏﹏ //

while (other, others) feel lonely even after a short time (alone, lonely).

   = other people   부사로 '홀로'

➜ 반면에 다른 사람들은 느낀다 / 외로움을 / 잠깐만 혼자 있어도

9 Some people (like, likes) spiders,

    주어가 복수

➜ ﹏﹏﹏﹏﹏﹏﹏ / 거미를 //

while others are afraid of (they, them).

    전치사 + 인칭대명사 목적격

➜ 반면에 다른 사람들은 ~이다 / 그것들을(거미를) 무서워하는

10 Some people enjoy (watching, to watch) scary movies *or (take, taking) roller coaster rides

       enjoy + 동사-ing   enjoy A or B

➜ 어떤 사람들은 즐긴다 / 무서운 영화를 보는 것이나 ﹏﹏﹏﹏﹏﹏ //

(so, because) they like the thrill of (feel, feeling) scared!

   이유나 원인   전치사 뒤에는 명사나 동명사

➜ 그들은 즐기기 때문에 / 무서운 기분의 전율을

등위 접속사 or

'또는', '혹은', '~이나'의 뜻을 가진 등위 접속사 or는 and와 마찬가지로 같은 품사끼리 연결해요.

- We might feel **happy or sad, excited or bored**. (형용사 + or + 형용사)
- Some people enjoy **watching scary movies or taking roller coaster rides**. (동명사 + or + 동명사)

Unit 09

Flowers

A **Speed Reading** 빠르게 읽으며 내용상 중요 단어나 구라고 생각되는 부분에 동그라미 하세요.

A flower is the part of a plant that produces fruit or seeds.
Flowers often have bright colors and a pleasant smell. To
make a seed, pollen from a stamen must land on a stigma.
This process is called pollination. It can occur between two different flowers or
within the same flower.

Flowers are pollinated in various ways. Some tiny pollen grains
are carried by the wind. Others attract insects with their color
and scent. Flowers also produce a sugary liquid called nectar.
While insects drink the nectar, pollen sticks to their bodies,
allowing them to carry it from flower to flower.

Words

pleasant 좋은 | pollen 꽃가루 (pollen grain 꽃가루 알갱이) | stamen 수술 | land 내려앉다, 착륙하다 | stigma 암술머리
process 과정, 처리하다 | pollination 수분 (pollinate 수분하다) | attract 끌어들이다 | insect 곤충 | sugary 설탕이 든, 달콤한
nectar 꽃의 꿀, 화밀 | stick 달라붙다

1   글의 내용과 일치하면 Yes, 틀리면 No에 동그라미 하세요.

1) A flower cannot make fruit or seeds.   **Yes**   **No**

2) Nectar helps pollination by insects.   **Yes**   **No**

3) The wind blows pollen from one flower to another.   **Yes**   **No**

2   글의 내용과 일치하도록 빈칸에 공통으로 들어갈 단어를 써 보세요. (서술형)

- ________________ is when pollen moves from a part of a flower to another, so the flower can make seeds.

- ________________ occurs within the same flower or between different flowers.

3   꽃의 수분을 돕는 2가지를 우리말로 써 보세요. (서술형)

→ ____

C   **C**hecking Vocabulary   단어를 영어로 바르게 설명한 것을 찾아 연결하세요.

1   pollen ●   ● ⓐ   the part of a flower that catches pollen

2   stamen ●   ● ⓑ   the sweet liquid a plant makes

3   stigma ●   ● ⓒ   the fine, yellow powder made by flowers

4   nectar ●   ● ⓓ   to cause people or animals to want to be near

5   attract ●   ● ⓔ   the part of a flower that produces pollen

Step **1.** 글의 내용을 생각하며 자세하게 다시 읽기
Step **2.** 빈칸을 채우며 문장 구조 생각하기

1 A flower is the part of a plant that produces fruit or seeds. **2** Flowers often have bright colors and a pleasant smell. **3** To make a seed, pollen from a stamen must land on a stigma. **4** This process is called pollination. **5** It can occur between two different flowers or within the same flower.

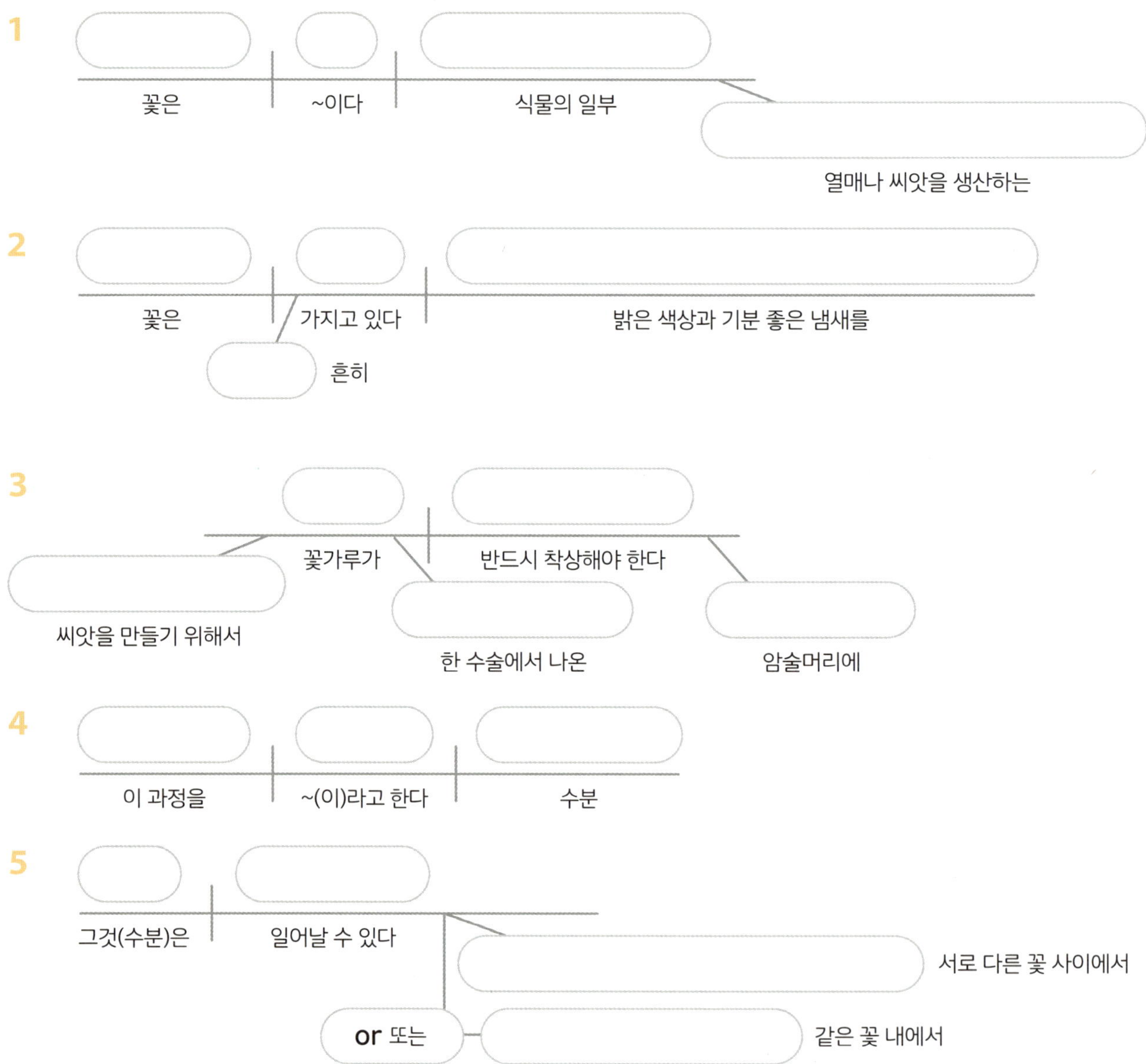

6 Flowers are pollinated in various ways. **7** Some tiny pollen grains are carried by the wind. **8** Others attract insects with their color and scent. **9** Flowers also produce a sugary liquid called nectar. **10** While insects drink the nectar, pollen sticks to their bodies, allowing them to carry it from flower to flower.

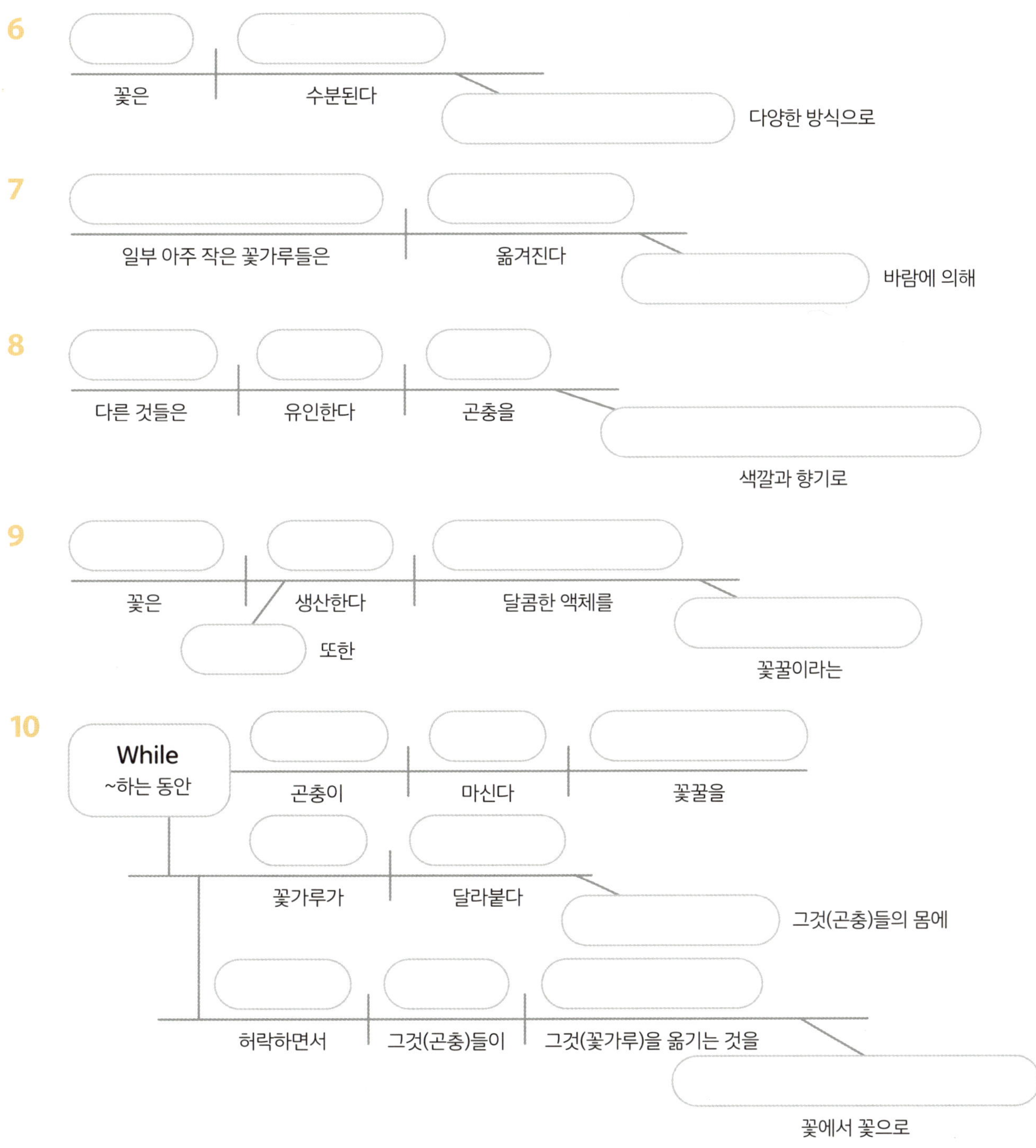

Step **1.** 괄호에서 문장의 흐름에 알맞은 단어나 표현 고르기
Step **2.** 해석에 맞게 끊어 읽기(/) 표시하며 문장을 읽고, 빈칸에 알맞은 해석 쓰기

TIP 읽기 속도를 높이기 위해 짧은 <(접속사 +) 주어 + 동사>는 한 덩어리로 읽기

1 A flower (is, are) the part (of, on) a plant that produces fruit or (seed, seeds).
주어가 단수 　　　~의 (일부) 　　　셀 수 있는 명사

→ 꽃은 ~이다 / ________________ / 열매나 씨앗을 생산하는

2 Flowers (have often, often have) bright colors and a pleasant (smell, smells).
빈도부사 + 일반동사 　　　a 뒤에는 단수명사

→ 꽃은 흔히 가지고 있다 / ________________ 기분 좋은 냄새를

3 To make a seed, pollen (to, from) a stamen must (land, landing) on a stigma.
~로부터 　　　조동사 must + 동사원형

→ ________________ / 수술에서 나온 꽃가루는 / 반드시 내려앉아야 한다 / 암술머리에

4 This process *is (call, called) pollination.
수동태는 be + 과거분사(p.p.)

→ 이 과정은 / ~라고 불린다 / ________________

5 It can (occur, occurs) between two different (flower, flowers) or within the same flower.
조동사 can + 동사원형 　　　two + 복수명사

→ 이것(수분)은 일어날 수 있다 / 서로 다른 두 꽃 사이에서 / 또는 ________________

6 Flowers *(is, are) pollinated (at, in) various ways.
주어가 복수 　　　in + 방식

→ 꽃은 수분된다 / ________________

7 Some tiny pollen (grain, grains) *are carried (at, by) the wind.
some + 셀 수 있는 명사 복수 　　　~에 의해

→ 일부 아주 작은 꽃가루들은 / 옮겨진다 / ________________

8 Others (attract, attracts) insects with (their, them) color and scent.

주어가 복수　　　　　　　　　소유격 + 명사

→ _____________ / 곤충을 / (그것들의) 색깔과 향기로

9 Flowers also (produce, produces) a (sugar, sugary) liquid called nectar.

주어가 복수　　　　a/an + 형용사 + 명사

→ _____________ / 달콤한 액체를 / 꿀꿀이라는

10 While insects (drink, drinks) the nectar,

주어가 복수

→ 곤충이 마시는 동안 / 꽃꿀을 //

pollen (stick, sticks) to (its, their) bodies,

주어가 단수　　　insects의 소유격

→ _____________ / 그것(곤충)들의 몸에 //

allowing them to carry it (to, from) flower (to, from) flower.

from A to B　　　　　from A to B

→ 허락하면서 / 그것(곤충)들이 / 그것(꽃가루)을 옮기도록 / _____________

수동태: be + 과거분사(p.p.)

능동태는 주어가 자발적으로 어떤 행위의 주체가 되는 경우예요. 반대로 수동태란 be동사 뒤에 과거분사가 오는 형태로 주어가 뭔가에 의해 어떤 행위의 대상이 되는 경우를 말해요. 예를 들어, '눈사람이 만들어졌다'처럼요. 수동태에서 사용되는 be동사는 주어의 수와 인칭에 맞춰 써요.

- This process **is called** pollination. (be + called: ~라 불리다)
- Flowers **are pollinated** in various ways. (be + pollinated: 수분되다)
- Some tiny pollen grains **are carried** by the wind. (be + carried: 옮겨지다)

Forest

A **Speed Reading** 빠르게 읽으며 내용상 중요 단어나 구라고 생각되는 부분에 동그라미 하세요.

A forest is a large area of land with many trees and plants. Forests cover more than 30 percent of the Earth's land. There are two main types of trees in forests: hardwoods and softwoods. Hardwoods have broad leaves, while softwoods have needle-shaped leaves and bear seeds in cones.

Forests are essential for living things. They provide food and shelter for birds and other animals. Forest trees increase the supply of oxygen. Forest soils act like giant sponges. They soak up rain, so it seeps slowly into the ground. Forests also provide timber for fuel, building houses, and making paper.

Words

hardwood 활엽수 **|** softwood 침엽수 **|** broad 넓은 **|** bear (열매를) 맺다, 낳다 **|** cone (소나무나 전나무의) 방울, 열매 **|** essential 필수적인
living things 생명체 **|** shelter 대피소, 주거지 **|** supply 공급(량) **|** soak up 빨아들이다 **|** seep 스며들다 **|** timber 목재 **|** fuel 연료

1 글의 내용과 일치하면 Yes, 틀리면 No에 동그라미 하세요.

1) Forests cover almost of the Earth's land. **Yes** **No**

2) Hardwoods have needle-shaped leaves. **Yes** **No**

3) Birds get food and shelter from forests. **Yes** **No**

2 글의 내용과 일치하도록 빈칸에 알맞은 단어를 써 보세요. (서술형)

A 1) f__________ provides food and 2) s__________ for living things. Trees in the forest also supply 3) o__________.

3 숲에 있는 나무의 대표적인 종류 2가지를 우리말로 써 보세요. (서술형)

➔

C **C**hecking Vocabulary 단어를 영어로 바르게 설명한 것을 찾아 연결하세요.

1 fuel • • ⓐ a place which is made to protect people or animals from bad weather or danger

2 seep • • ⓑ an amount of something which someone has or which is available for them to use

3 shelter • • ⓒ anything such as wood or gasoline that is burned to provide heat or power

4 supply • • ⓓ wood that is used for building houses and making furniture

5 timber • • ⓔ to spread or flow through gradually

Step **1.** 글의 내용을 생각하며 자세하게 다시 읽기
Step **2.** 빈칸을 채우며 문장 구조 생각하기

1 A forest is a large area of land with many trees and plants. **2** Forests cover more than 30 percent of the Earth's land. **3** There are two main types of trees in forests: hardwoods and softwoods. **4** Hardwoods have broad leaves, while softwoods have needle-shaped leaves and bear seeds in cones.

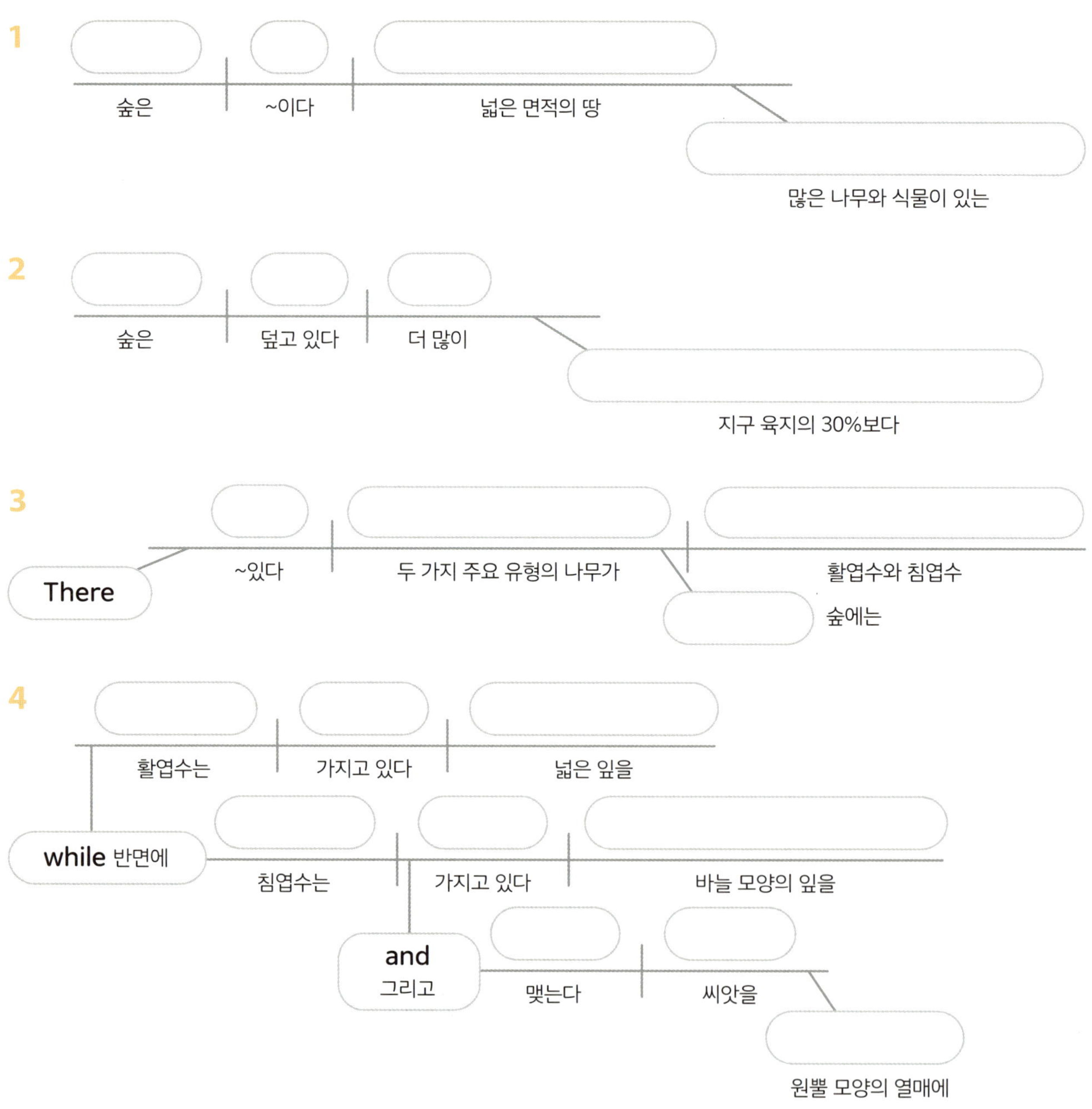

5 Forests are essential for living things. 6 They provide food and shelter for birds and other animals. 7 Forest trees increase the supply of oxygen. 8 Forest soils act like giant sponges. 9 They soak up rain, so it seeps slowly into the ground. 10 Forests also provide timber for fuel, building houses, and making paper.

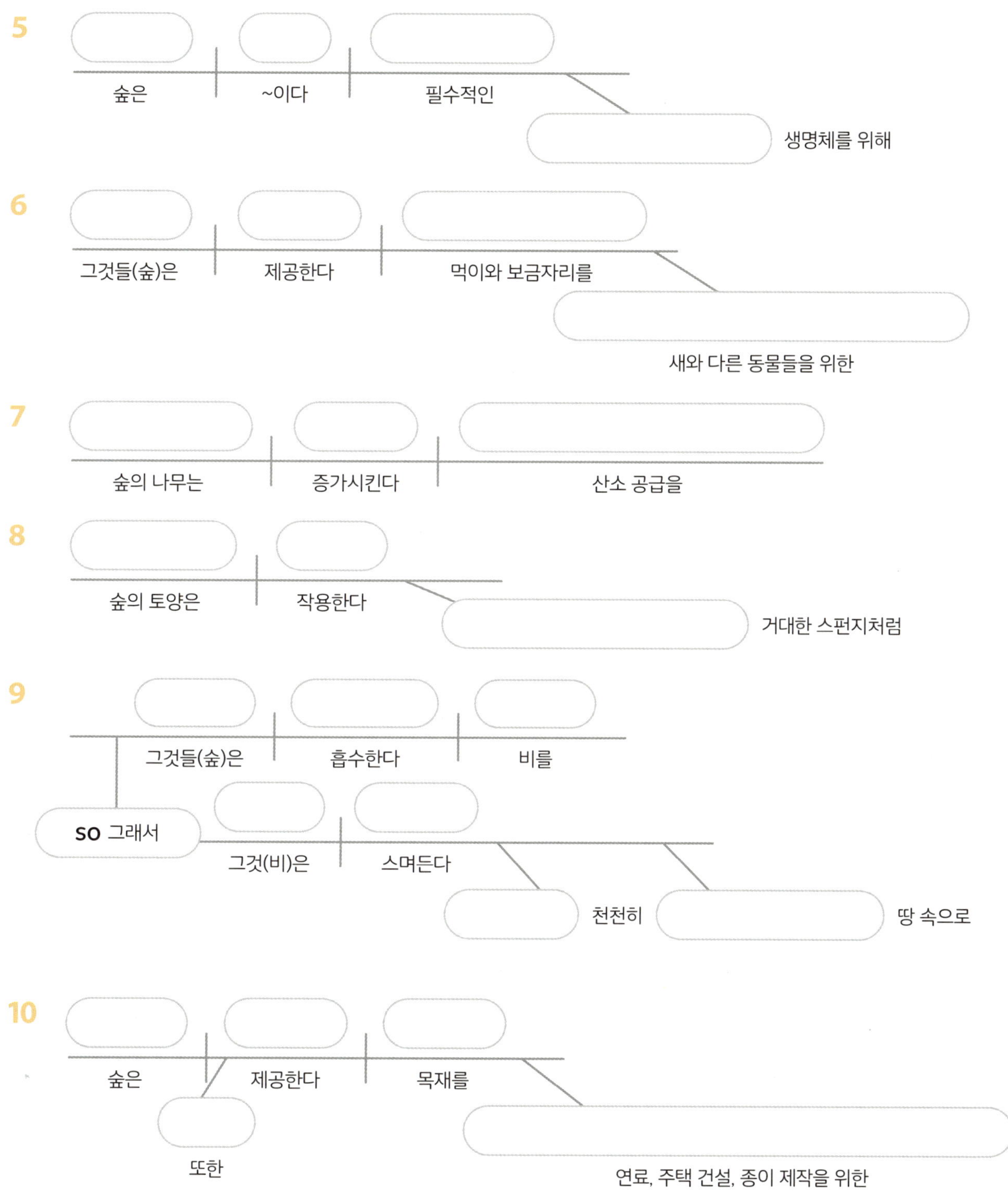

Grammar for Reading

Step **1.** 괄호에서 문장의 흐름에 알맞은 단어나 표현 고르기
Step **2.** 해석에 맞게 끊어 읽기(/) 표시하며 문장을 읽고, 빈칸에 알맞은 해석 쓰기

TIP 읽기 속도를 높이기 위해 짧은 <(접속사 +) 주어 + 동사>는 한 덩어리로 읽기

1 *(A forest, Forests) is a large area of *land with *many (tree, trees) and plants.
동사가 3인칭 단수 동사   many + 복수명사

→ 숲은 ~이다 / 넓은 면적의 땅 / ____________ 이 있는

2 Forests (cover, covers) more (to, than) 30 percent of the Earth's land.
주어가 복수   비교급: ~보다

→ 숲은 덮고 있다 / ~보다 더 많이 / ____________ 30%

3 There (is, are) two main *types of trees (at, in) forests: hardwoods (or, and) softwoods.
주어가 복수인 types   ~ 안에   등위접속사: ~와

→ ~있다 / 두 가지 주요 유형의 나무가 / 숲에는 / ____________

4 *Hardwoods (has, have) broad (leafs, leaves),
주어가 복수   f로 끝나는 단어의 복수형

→ 활엽수는 가지고 있다 / ____________ //

(because, while) softwoods have needle-shaped leaves and (bear, bears) seeds in cones.
활엽수와 침엽수를 대조   주어가 복수

→ 반면에 침엽수는 가지고 있다 / ____________ / 그리고 맺는다 / 씨앗을 / 원뿔 모양의 열매에

5 Forests (is, are) essential (with, for) living things.
주어가 복수   ~을 위해

→ 숲은 ~이다 / ____________ / 생명체를 위해

6 They provide *(food, foods) and shelter for (bird, birds) and other animals.
food는 셀 수 없는 명사   bird는 셀 수 있는 명사

→ 그것들(숲)은 제공한다 / ____________ / 새와 다른 동물들을 위한

7 Forest trees (increase, increases) the supply (of, to) oxygen.

주어가 복수　　　　　　　　　　～의(~와 관련된)

➜ 숲의 나무는 증가시킨다 / ＿＿＿＿＿＿＿＿＿＿

8 Forest soils (act, acts) like giant (sponge, sponges).

주어가 복수　　　　　　　　sponge는 셀 수 있는 명사

➜ 숲의 토양은 작용한다 / ＿＿＿＿＿＿＿＿＿＿

9 They soak up *rain, (so, so that) it seeps (slow, slowly) into the ground.

그래서　　　　　　　　앞의 동사를 수식하는 부사

➜ 그것들(숲)은 흡수한다 / 비를 / 그래서 그것(비)은 스며든다 / 천천히 / ＿＿＿＿＿＿＿

10 Forests also provide timber (for, to) fuel, (build, building) houses, and making paper.

～을 위해(목적)　　　나열할 때는 같은 품사로(전치사 + 명사/동명사)

➜ 숲은 또한 제공한다 / ＿＿＿＿＿＿＿＿＿ / 연료, 주택 건설, 종이 제작을 위한

셀 수 있는 명사

셀 수 있는 명사가 하나인 단수명사 앞에는 a나 an을 써요. 둘 이상인 복수명사는 끝에 -s 또는 -es를 붙이거나 불규칙 복수형으로 써야 해요. some/any, many/a lot of 뒤에 셀 수 있는 명사가 오면 복수로 써요.

- A **forest** is ⋯⋯ with many **trees** and **plants**.
- There are two main **types** of **trees**.
- **Hardwoods** have broad **leaves**.

셀 수 없는 명사

셀 수 없는 명사는 a나 an을 함께 쓰지 않고, 복수형이 없어요. some/any, much/a lot of 뒤에 올 때도 단수로 써요.

- A forest is a large area of **land**.
- They provide **food** and **shelter**.
- They soak up **rain**.

Unit 11 — Friends

A **Speed Reading** 빠르게 읽으며 내용상 중요 단어나 구라고 생각되는 부분에 동그라미 하세요.

A friend is someone we know, like, and trust. It is a special feeling to have a good friend and to be one. Friends usually have a lot in common. This helps us understand each other and have fun together. Friends enjoy doing things together and helping each other.

However, friends can be quite different from one another. Elderly people can be friends with younger people. You may find a friend after talking to or playing with someone a few times. You may argue, but you do not stop caring. True friends understand us and help us grow. Friends are the family we choose.

Words

trust 신뢰하다 **ㅣ** in common 공통적인, 공동으로 **ㅣ** understand 이해하다 **ㅣ** be different from ~와 다르다 **ㅣ** one another 서로
elderly 연세 드신 **ㅣ** argue 언쟁을 하다 **ㅣ** care 관심을 가지다, 돌보다 **ㅣ** choose 선택하다

1   글의 내용과 일치하면 Yes, 틀리면 No에 동그라미 하세요.

1) Friends should be very different.   **Yes**   **No**

2) Friends can be the family.   **Yes**   **No**

3) Only people of the same age can be friends.   **Yes**   **No**

2   글의 내용과 일치하도록 빈칸에 알맞은 단어를 써 보세요. (서술형)

Because friends usually have a lot in 1) c__________, they 2) u__________ each other and have 3) f__________ together.

3   친구를 찾을 수 있는 2가지 방법을 우리말로 써 보세요. (서술형)

→ ____

C   **C**hecking Vocabulary   단어를 영어로 바르게 설명한 것을 찾아 연결하세요.

1   understand ●   ● ⓐ   to feel affection toward someone

2   common ●   ● ⓑ   to get the meaning of; to know very well the ways and nature of

3   care ●   ● ⓒ   shared with another or others

4   argue ●   ● ⓓ   old or aging

5   elderly ●   ● ⓔ   to express disagreement; to quarrel

Step **1.** 글의 내용을 생각하며 자세하게 다시 읽기
Step **2.** 빈칸을 채우며 문장 구조 생각하기

1 A friend is someone we know, like, and trust. **2** It is a special feeling to have a good friend and to be one. **3** Friends usually have a lot in common. **4** This helps us understand each other and have fun together. **5** Friends enjoy doing things together and helping each other.

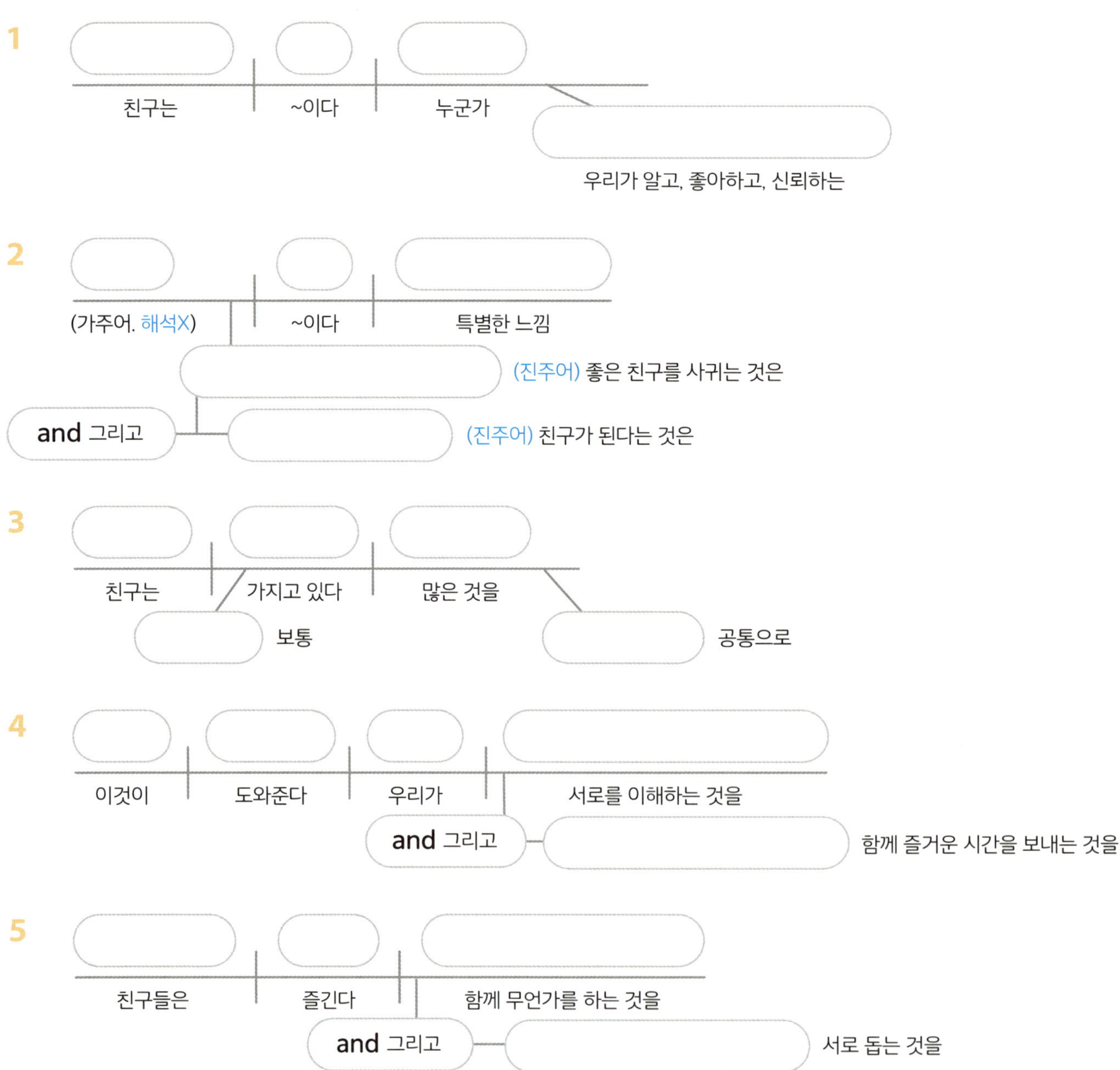

6 However, friends can be quite different from one another. **7** Elderly people can be friends with younger people. **8** You may find a friend after talking to or playing with someone a few times. **9** You may argue, but you do not stop caring. **10** True friends understand us and help us grow. **11** Friends are the family we choose.

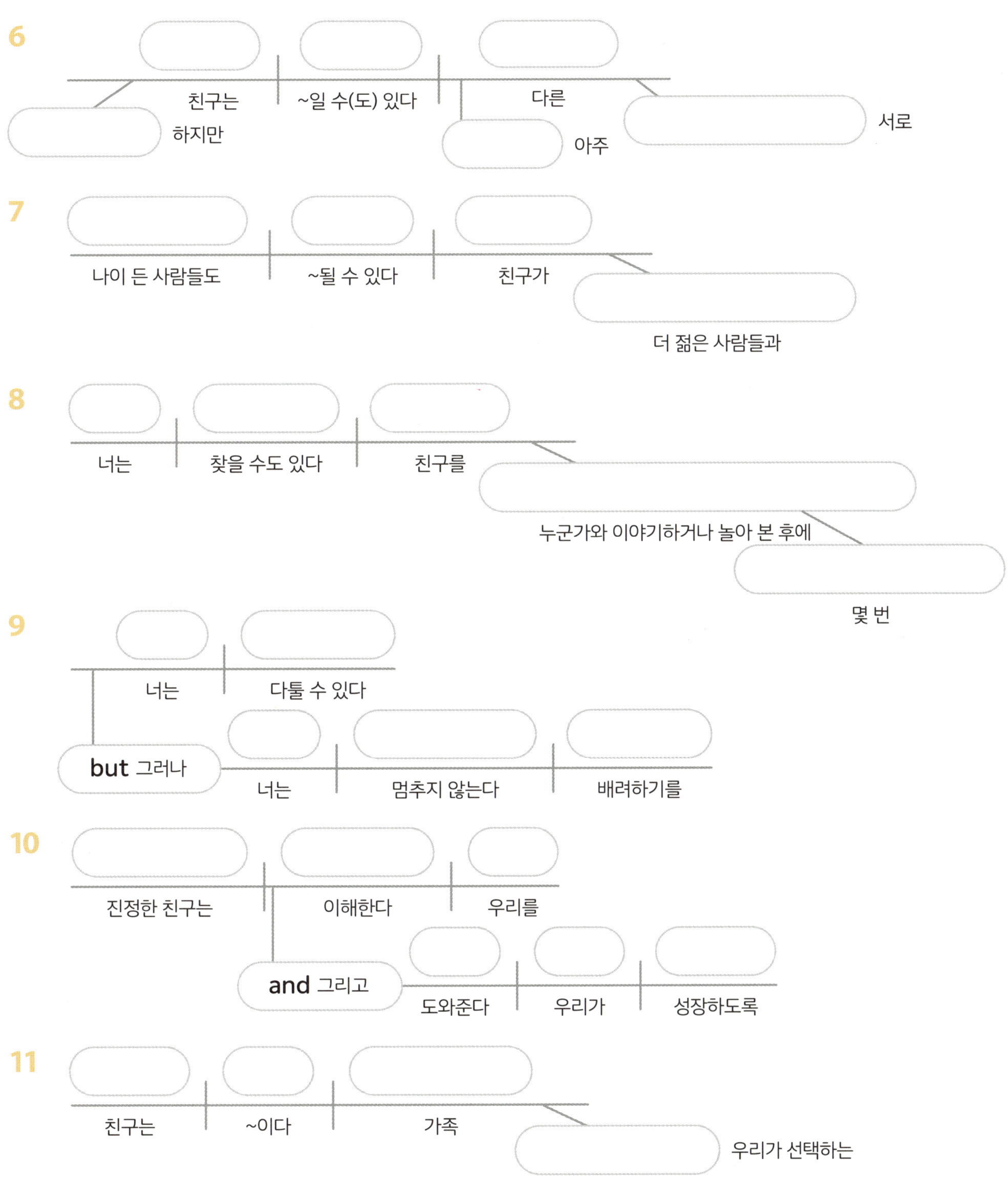

Step **1.** 괄호에서 문장의 흐름에 알맞은 단어나 표현 고르기
Step **2.** 해석에 맞게 끊어 읽기(/) 표시하며 문장을 읽고, 빈칸에 알맞은 해석 쓰기

TIP 읽기 속도를 높이기 위해 짧은 <(접속사 +) 주어 + 동사>는 한 덩어리로 읽기

1 A friend (is, have) someone we know, like, *and (trust, trusting).
주어가 단수   and는 같은 품사 단어끼리 연결

→ 친구는 ~이다 / 누군가 / ____________ , 좋아하고, 신뢰하는

2 (It, This) is a special feeling to have a good friend *and (being, to be) one.
It 가주어, to do 진주어   and는 같은 형태 단어끼리 연결

→ ~이다 / 특별한 느낌 / 좋은 친구를 사귀는 것은 / 그리고 ____________

3 Friends (usually have, have usually) a lot in common.
빈도부사는 일반동사 앞에

→ 친구는 보통 가지고 있다 / 많은 것을 / ____________

4 This helps (we, us) understand each other *and (have, having) fun together.
동사의 목적어   understand와 and로 연결

→ 이는 도와준다 / 우리가 / ____________ / 그리고 함께 즐겁게 지내도록

5 Friends (enjoy, enjoys) doing things together* and (help, helping) each other.
주어가 복수   enjoy + 동사-ing

→ ____________ / 무언가 함께 하는 것을 / 그리고 서로 돕는 것을

6 However, friends can (be, are) quite different (from, to) one another.
조동사 + 동사원형   ~와 다른

→ 하지만 / 친구는 ~일 수 있다 / ____________ / 서로

7 Elderly people can be friends (with, from) younger people.
~와

→ 나이 든 사람들도 / ~될 수 있다 / 친구가 / ____________

8 You may (find, found) a friend after (talk, talking) to or playing (with, to) someone
　　조동사 + 동사원형　　　　　　전치사 + 동명사　　　　　　　　~와

a few times.

→ ＿＿＿＿＿＿＿＿＿＿＿ / 친구를 / 누군가와 이야기하거나 놀다 보면 / 몇 번

9 You may argue, but you (do, are) not stop (care, caring).
　　　　　　　일반동사의 부정　　　　stop + 동사-ing

→ 너는 다툴 수 있다 / 하지만 ＿＿＿＿＿＿＿＿＿＿＿ / 신경 쓰는 것을

10 True friends (understand, understands) us *and help us (grow, growing).
　　　　　　　　주어가 복수　　　　　　　help + 목적어 + 목적 보어(동사원형)

→ ＿＿＿＿＿＿＿＿＿＿＿ / 우리를 / 그리고 도와준다 / 우리가 / 성장하도록

11 Friends (is, are) the family we choose.
　　　　주어가 복수

→ 친구는 ~이다 / 가족 / ＿＿＿＿＿＿＿＿＿＿＿

등위 접속사 and

'~와', '그리고'의 뜻을 가진 등위 접속사 and는 같은 품사의 단어나 대등한 관계에 있는 구나 절을 연결해요. 연결되는 것이 세 개 이상이면 콤마(,)를 사용하여 연결하고, 마지막 대상 바로 앞에 접속사 and를 써요.

- A friend is someone we know, like, **and** trust.
  (3개 이상의 동사를 연결)
- It is a special feeling to have a good friend **and** to be one.
  (to 부정사 + and + to 부정사)
- This helps us understand each other **and** have fun together.
  (동사원형 + and + 동사원형)
- Friends enjoy doing things together **and** helping each other.
  (동명사 + and + 동명사)
- True friends understand us **and** help us grow.
  (동사원형 + and + 동사원형)

Kangaroos

A **Speed Reading** 빠르게 읽으며 내용상 중요 단어나 구라고 생각되는 부분에 동그라미 하세요.

A kangaroo is a large Australian animal that moves by jumping on its back legs. It is a plant-eating animal with large ears, strong back legs, short front legs, and a long tail. A kangaroo can run up to 30 miles an hour. As it runs, it holds up its thick tail for balance.

A female kangaroo has a big pouch in the front of her body, where her baby grows. The baby spends about six months inside the pouch. It continues to drink its mother's milk until it is a year old. Male kangaroos fight each other to decide who is boss. The winner becomes the leader of the group.

Words

Australian 호주의 ｜ plant-eating 초식(의) ｜ hold up 들어 올리다, 떠받치다 ｜ balance 균형 ｜ female 암컷(의), 여성(인) ｜ pouch 주머니, 새끼주머니
continue 계속하다 ｜ male 수컷(의), 남성(인) ｜ boss 우두머리 ｜ winner 승자

1   글의 내용과 일치하면 Yes, 틀리면 No에 동그라미 하세요.

    1) A kangaroo jumps on its short legs.   **Yes**   **No**

    2) A kangaroo usually eats plants.   **Yes**   **No**

    3) A male kangaroo has a pouch.   **Yes**   **No**

2   글의 내용과 일치하도록 빈칸에 알맞은 단어를 써 보세요. (서술형)

    A baby kangaroo grows in the mother's 1) p__________ and drinks 2) m__________
    from its mother.

3   캥거루의 굵고 긴 꼬리가 하는 역할을 쓰세요. (서술형)

→ ～～～～～～～～～～～～～～～～～～～～～～～～～～～～～～～～～～～～～

C   **Checking Vocabulary**   단어를 영어로 바르게 설명한 것을 찾아 연결하세요.

1   boss   ●   ●   ⓐ   to keep happening, to go on with

2   balance   ●   ●   ⓑ   the one who leads a group and make decisions

3   female   ●   ●   ⓒ   the way to keep your body steady so you don't fall

4   pouch   ●   ●   ⓓ   a person or animal of the sex that can have babies
    or young; a woman or girl

5   continue   ●   ●   ⓔ   a natural pocket of skin in some female animals
    that is used to hold and carry young

Step **1.** 글의 내용을 생각하며 자세하게 다시 읽기
Step **2.** 빈칸을 채우며 문장 구조 생각하기

1 A kangaroo is a large Australian animal that moves by jumping on its back legs. **2** It is a plant-eating animal with large ears, strong back legs, short front legs, and a long tail. **3** A kangaroo can run up to 30 miles an hour. **4** As it runs, it holds up its thick tail for balance.

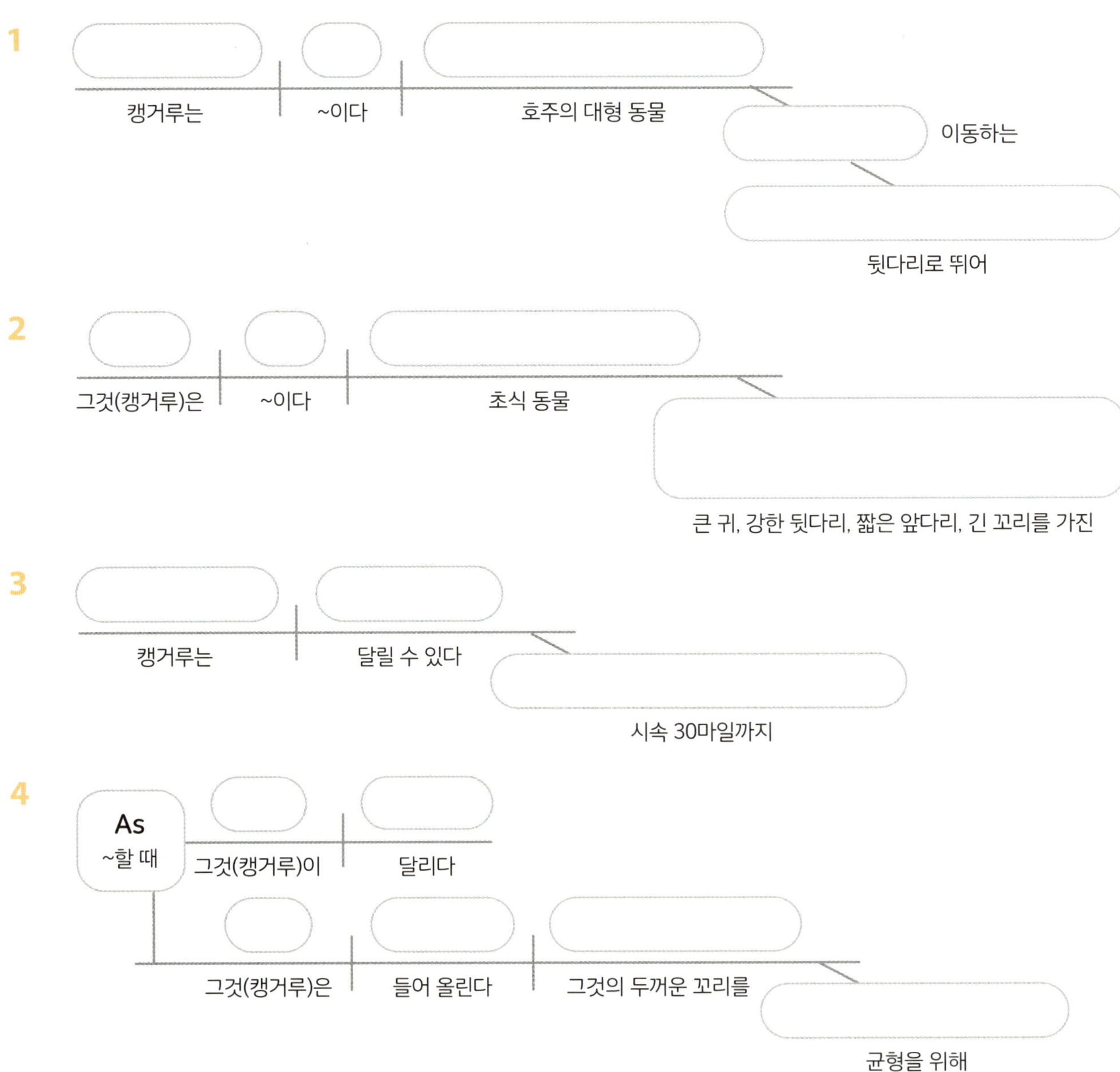

5 A female kangaroo has a big pouch in the front of her body, where her baby grows.
6 The baby spends about six months inside the pouch. **7** It continues to drink its mother's milk until it is a year old. **8** Male kangaroos fight each other to decide who is boss. **9** The winner becomes the leader of the group.

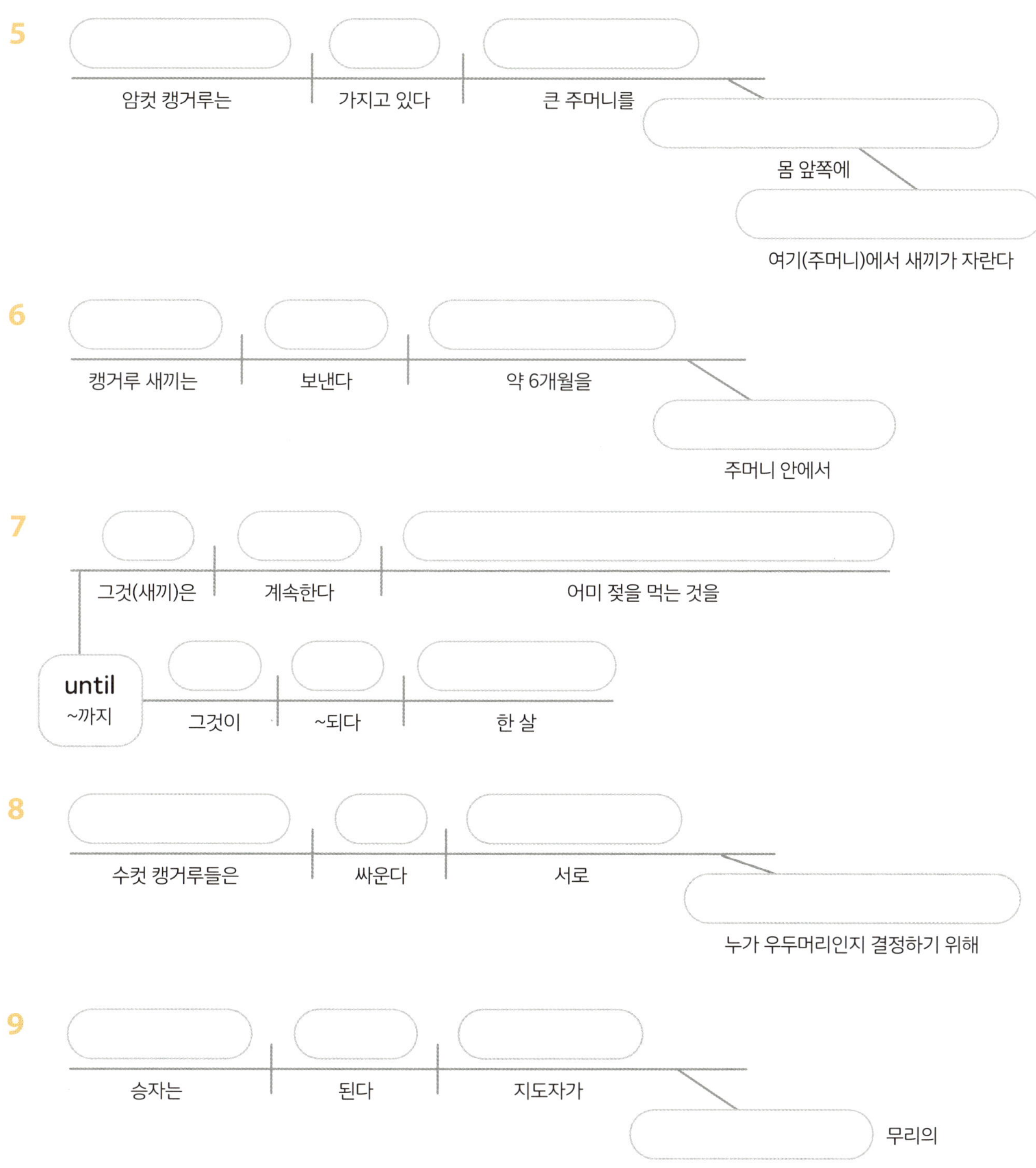

5
암컷 캥거루는
가지고 있다
큰 주머니를
몸 앞쪽에
여기(주머니)에서 새끼가 자란다

6
캥거루 새끼는
보낸다
약 6개월을
주머니 안에서

7
그것(새끼)은
계속한다
어미 젖을 먹는 것을
until
~까지
그것이
~되다
한 살

8
수컷 캥거루들은
싸운다
서로
누가 우두머리인지 결정하기 위해

9
승자는
된다
지도자가
무리의

Step **1.** 괄호에서 문장의 흐름에 알맞은 단어나 표현 고르기
Step **2.** 해석에 맞게 끊어 읽기(/) 표시하며 문장을 읽고, 빈칸에 알맞은 해석 쓰기

TIP 읽기 속도를 높이기 위해 짧은 <(접속사 +) 주어 + 동사>는 한 덩어리로 읽기

1　A kangaroo (is, are) a large Australian animal
주어가 단수

→ 캥거루는 ~이다 / ________________ //

*that (move, moves) by (jump, jumping) on its back legs.
선행사 animal이 단수　　　전치사 by + 명사 또는 동명사

→ 이동하는 / __________ 뛰어서

2　It is (a, some) plant-eating animal (for, with) large ears, strong back (leg, legs),
단수명사 앞　　　　　　　　　　　~을 가진　　　　　　　　　의미상 복수

short front legs, (but, and) a long (tail, tails).
나열하는 마지막 단어 앞　　a + 셀 수 있는 단수명사

→ 그것은 ~이다 / 초식동물 / __________________________________, 긴 꼬리를 가진

3　A kangaroo (can run, can runs) up to 30 miles (a, an) hour.
조동사 + 동사원형　　　　　　hour의 첫소리는 묵음

→ __________________ / 시속 30마일까지

4　(As, Because) it runs, it (hold, holds) up its thick tail (by, for) balance.
~할 때　　　　　　주어가 단수　　　　　~을 위해(목적)

→ 그것(캥거루)은 달릴 때, / 그것은 들어 올린다 / __________ / 균형을 잡기 위해

5　A (woman, female) kangaroo has a big pouch (on, in) the front of (his, her) body,
동물에도 사용할 수 있는 표현　　　　　　　　　~ 앞에　　　　주어로 나온 암컷을 말함

→ 암컷 캥거루는 가지고 있다 / __________ / 몸 앞쪽에 //

(where, when) her baby (grow, grows).
pouch 장소를 의미　　　　　주어가 단수

→ 여기(주머니)에서 __________

6 The baby (spend, spends) about six (month, months) inside the pouch.
　　　　　　　주어가 단수　　　　　　　　　　　six 뒤에는 복수명사

→ 캥거루 새끼는 보낸다 / ＿＿＿＿＿＿＿＿ / 주머니 안에서

7 It continues (drink, to drink) its mother's milk until it is a (year, years) old.
　　　　　동사의 목적어 to 부정사　　　　　　　　　　　한 살: a + 단수명사

→ 그것은 계속한다 / 어미 젖을 먹는 것을 / ＿＿＿＿＿＿＿＿

8 Male kangaroos (fight, fights) each other (decide, to decide) who (is, are) boss.
　　　　　　주어가 복수　　　　　　~하기 위해서(목적)　　의문사 주어는 단수 취급

→ 수컷 캥거루들은 싸운다 / 서로 / ＿＿＿＿＿＿ 결정하기 위해

9 The winner (become, becomes) the leader (of, to) the group.
　　　　　주어가 단수　　　　　　~의(소속)

→ ＿＿＿＿＿＿＿＿ / 지도자가 / 무리의

관계대명사의 선행사

두 문장을 이을 때 뒤 문장의 대명사를 대신하는 앞 문장의 명사를 '선행사'라고 해요. 관계대명사의 동사 형태는 선행사가 단수인지 복수인지에 따라 결정해요.

- A kangaroo is a large Australian animal. + It moves by jumping on its back legs.
  → A kangaroo is a large Australian animal **that moves** by jumping on its back legs.

1) 두 문장을 하나로 만들기 위해 두 문장의 공통 요소인 animal을 대신하는 주어 It을 생략했어요.
2) 단어가 생략된 자리에는 관계대명사 that을 쓰고 앞의 선행사에 맞춰 단수동사를 써요.
3) 뒤의 문장은 앞 문장 선행사에 대한 추가적인 정보를 주는 역할로, '뒷다리로 뛰어서 이동하는'이라고 해석해요.

Unit 13 — Learning

A **Speed Reading** 빠르게 읽으며 내용상 중요 단어나 구라고 생각되는 부분에 동그라미 하세요.

Learning is the process of finding out about things. It helps you understand the world around you. It leads to personal growth and development. You can learn new knowledge, skills, attitudes, or behaviors. There are different ways to learn. You can learn by experience, study, or teaching, and even by making mistakes.

Learning takes place all the time. You can learn to do some things very quickly. More difficult skills, such as reading or writing, can take much longer and may require help. Learning is a lifelong journey. You will continue to learn all kinds of things throughout your life. The more you learn, the more interesting life becomes.

Words

find out 알아내다 l **personal** 개인의 l **growth** 성장 l **development** 발달, 성장 l **knowledge** 지식 l **attitude** 태도 l **behavior** 행동
take place 일어나다(= happen) l **require** 요구하다 l **lifelong** 평생의, 일생의

B **Reading for Information** 글을 빠르게 다시 읽고, 아래 질문에 답하세요.

1 글의 내용과 일치하면 Yes, 틀리면 No에 동그라미 하세요.

1) You cannot learn by making mistakes. **Yes** **No**

2) Learning helps you grow and develop. **Yes** **No**

3) Learning happens only during childhood. **Yes** **No**

2 글의 내용과 일치하도록 빈칸에 공통으로 들어갈 단어를 써 보세요. (서술형)

- You can ___________ all the time and throughout your life.

- You can ___________ by experience, study, or teaching, and making mistakes.

3 새로운 지식 외에도 우리가 배울 수 있는 것 3가지를 찾아 우리말로 써 보세요. (서술형)

→ ____

C **Checking Vocabulary** 단어를 영어로 바르게 설명한 것을 찾아 연결하세요.

1 process • • ⓐ going on throughout the whole of a person's life

2 attitude • • ⓑ a long trip from one place to another

3 mistake • • ⓒ a series of actions for doing something or reaching a goal

4 lifelong • • ⓓ a way of feeling or thinking about something or someone

5 journey • • ⓔ a thought or action that is not correct; error

Step **1.** 글의 내용을 생각하며 자세하게 다시 읽기
Step **2.** 빈칸을 채우며 문장 구조 생각하기

1 Learning is the process of finding out about things. **2** It helps you understand the world around you. **3** It leads to personal growth and development. **4** You can learn new knowledge, skills, attitudes, or behaviors. **5** There are different ways to learn. **6** You can learn by experience, study, or teaching, and even by making mistakes.

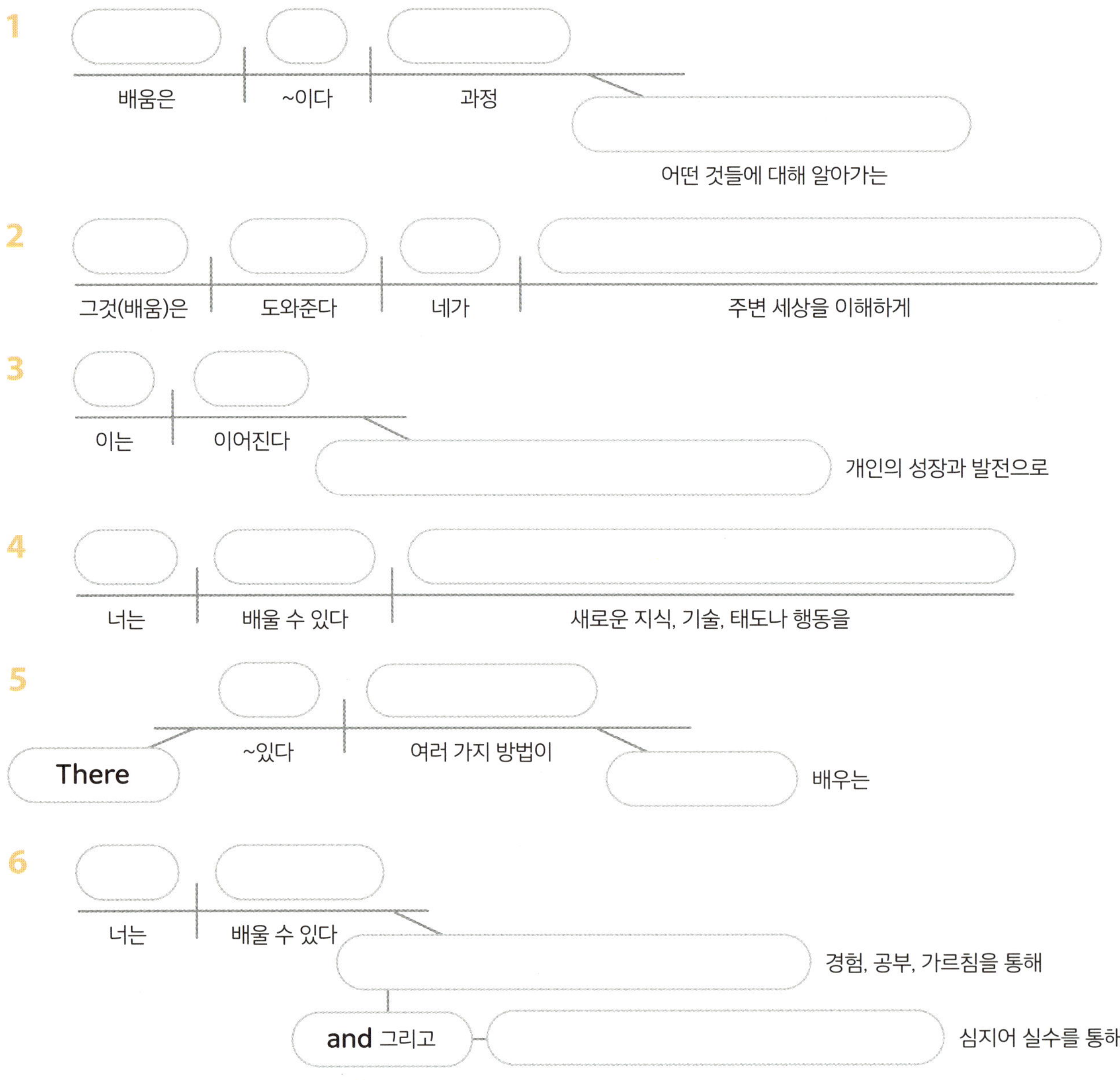

7 Learning takes place all the time. 8 You can learn to do some things very quickly. 9 More difficult skills, such as reading or writing, can take much longer and may require help. 10 Learning is a lifelong journey. 11 You will continue to learn all kinds of things throughout your life. 12 The more you learn, the more interesting life becomes.

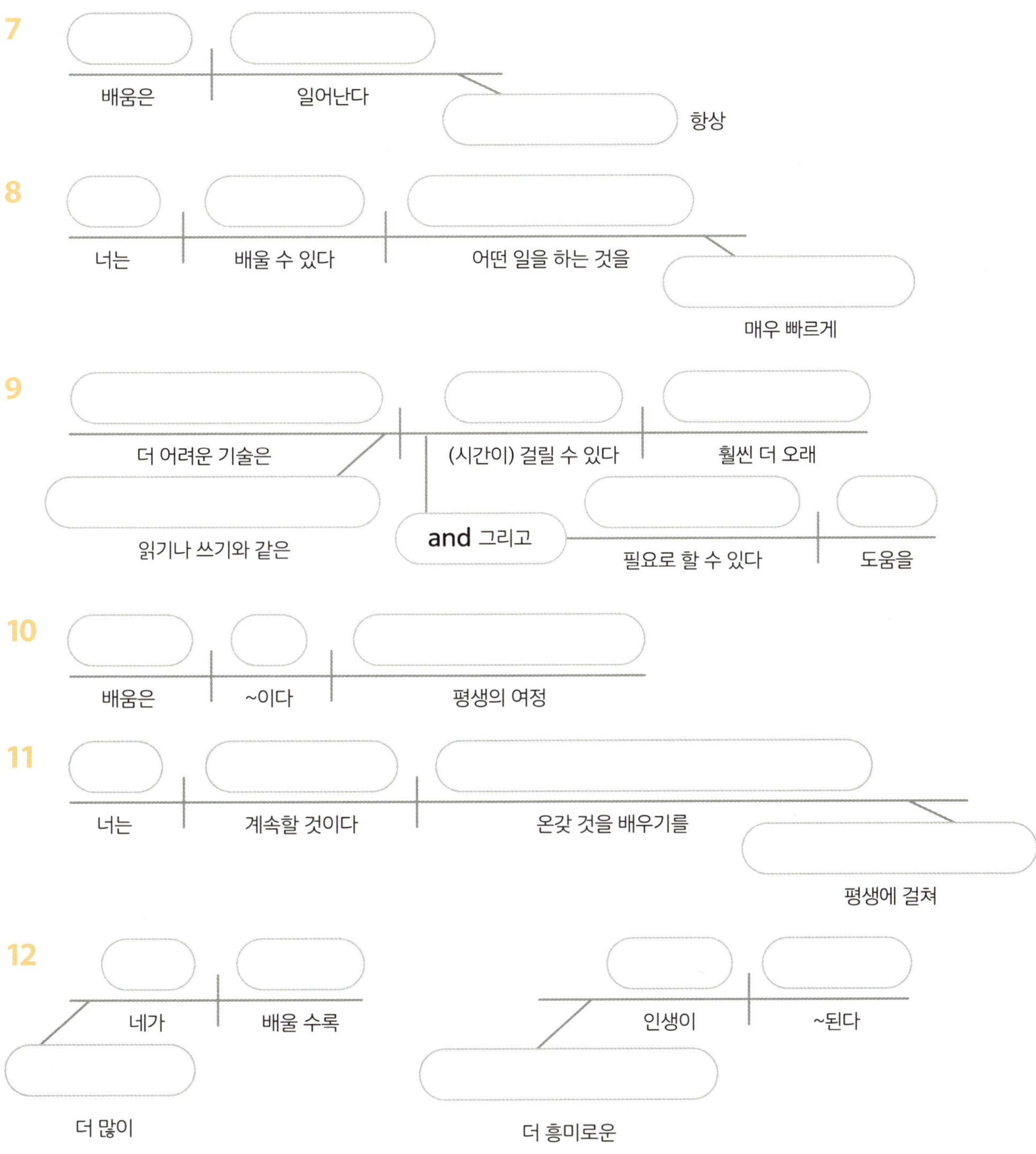

7
배움은
일어난다
항상

8
너는
배울 수 있다
어떤 일을 하는 것을
매우 빠르게

9
더 어려운 기술은
(시간이) 걸릴 수 있다
훨씬 더 오래
읽기나 쓰기와 같은
and 그리고
필요로 할 수 있다
도움을

10
배움은
~이다
평생의 여정

11
너는
계속할 것이다
온갖 것을 배우기를
평생에 걸쳐

12
네가
배울 수록
인생이
~된다
더 많이
더 흥미로운

E Grammar for Reading

Step **1**. 괄호에서 문장의 흐름에 알맞은 단어나 표현 고르기
Step **2**. 해석에 맞게 끊어 읽기(/) 표시하며 문장을 읽고, 빈칸에 알맞은 해석 쓰기

TIP 읽기 속도를 높이기 위해 짧은 <(접속사 +) 주어 + 동사>는 한 덩어리로 읽기

1 (Learn, Learning) is the process of (find, finding) out about things.
  주어 자리에 오는 품사 　　　　　　　　전치사 of + 명사 또는 동명사

  → 배움은 ~이다 / 과정 / ______________ 알아가는

2 It helps you (understand, understanding) the world around you.
  　　　　help + 목적어 + 목적 보어(동사원형)

  → 그것은 도와준다 / 네가 / 주변의 ______________

3 (It, They) leads to personal (growth, grow) and development.
  앞 문장의 Learning을 대신 　　　　전치사 to + 명사

  → ______________ / 개인의 성장과 발전으로

4 You can learn new knowledge, skills, attitudes, (or, but) behaviors.
  　　　　　　　　　　세 개 이상의 대상을 연결하는 접속사

  → ______________ / 새로운 지식, 기술, 태도나 행동을

5 There (is, are) different ways (learning, to learn).
  　　주어가 복수 　　　　앞의 명사 ways를 수식(형용사 역할)

  → ~있다 / ______________ / 배우는

6 You can learn by experience, study, teaching, and even by (making, make) mistakes.
  　　　　　　　　　　　　　　전치사 by + 명사 또는 동명사

  → 너는 배울 수 있다 / ______________ / 그리고 심지어 실수를 통해

7 Learning (take place, takes place) all the time.
  　　　　동명사 주어는 단수

  → 배움은 일어난다 / ______________

8 You can learn (to do, doing) some things very (quick, quickly).

learn + to do(목적어)   동사 learn을 수식하는 부사

→ 너는 배울 수 있다 / 어떤 일을 하는 것을 / ＿＿＿＿＿＿＿＿

9 (More difficult, Difficulter) skills, such as reading or (write, writing), can take

2음절 이상 형용사 비교급   접속사 or 앞뒤로 같은 품사

→ 더 어려운 기술은 / ＿＿＿＿＿＿＿＿＿＿ / 걸릴 수 있다 //

much (more long, longer) and may (require, requires) help.

1음절 형용사 비교급   조동사 + 동사원형

→ 더 오래 / 그리고 ＿＿＿＿＿＿＿＿ / 도움을

10 Learning (is, are) a lifelong journey.

동명사 주어는 단수

→ 배움은 ~이다 / ＿＿＿＿＿＿＿＿

11 You will continue to learn all (kinds, kind) of things throughout (you, your) life.

all + 셀 수 있는 명사 복수형   일생을 통하여: throughout one's life

→ 너는 계속할 것이다 / 온갖 것을 배우기를 / ＿＿＿＿＿＿＿＿

12 *The (much, more) you learn, the (better, more) interesting life becomes.

the 비교급, the 비교급   the 비교급, the 비교급

→ ＿＿＿＿＿＿ / 네가 배울수록 / 더 흥미로운 / 인생이 된다

the 비교급, the 비교급

비교급을 이용한 표현으로 '더 ~할수록, 더 …하다'의 뜻이에요. 이 표현은 비교급 앞에 정관사 the를 붙이고, 비교급을 문장 앞으로 보내요.

- You learn **more**. Life becomes **more interesting**.
  ⇒ (비교급 강조 문장) 형용사나 부사의 비교급 앞에 the를 붙여서 '주어 + 동사' 앞으로 이동시킴.
    The more you learn, **the more interesting** life becomes.

- **The more** you get, **the more** you want. 가지면 가질수록 더 갖고 싶어진다. (서양 속담)

Movement

A **Speed Reading** 빠르게 읽으며 내용상 중요 단어나 구라고 생각되는 부분에 동그라미 하세요.

You can walk, run, stretch, and dance by moving your body. Motor nerves allow the brain to control your muscles. Thousands of muscles are attached to your bones. When you want to move, your brain figures out which muscles are needed. Then, the brain sends messages to these muscles, telling them to move your bones.

The human brain has more than 100 billion nerve cells. The front part of the brain plans and makes decisions. It does this by processing the different types of information received from nerve cells. This information is called sensory information. It comes from your senses, such as sight, hearing, touch, taste, and smell.

Words

stretch 늘이다, 뻗다 **|** motor nerve 운동 신경 (nerve 신경) **|** control 제어하다 **|** muscle 근육 **|** attach 붙이다 **|** figure out 생각해 내다, 이해하다
make a decision 결정을 내리다 **|** sensory 감각의 (sense 감각) **|** sight 시각, 시력

B **Reading for Information** 글을 빠르게 다시 읽고, 아래 질문에 답하세요.

1 글의 내용과 일치하면 Yes, 틀리면 No에 동그라미 하세요.

1) The brain controls your muscles. **Yes** **No**

2) The human brain has 10 billion nerve cells. **Yes** **No**

3) The back part of the brain makes decisions. **Yes** **No**

2 글의 내용과 일치하도록 빈칸에 알맞은 단어를 써 보세요. (서술형)

Thousands of 1) m__________ are attached to your bones. The 2) b__________ sends signals to these muscles, causing them to move your bones.

3 감각 기관을 통해 얻는 정보를 무엇이라 하는지 영어로 써 보세요. (서술형)

➔

C **Checking Vocabulary** 단어를 영어로 바르게 설명한 것을 찾아 연결하세요.

1 nerve • • ⓐ the organ inside your head that controls your whole body and lets you think, feel and remember

2 brain • • ⓑ long and thin thread in your body that carry messages between the brain and other parts of the body

3 muscle • • ⓒ the parts inside your body that you use when you move

4 attach • • ⓓ the act or result of making up one's mind

5 decision • • ⓔ to join, fasten, or connect

Step **1.** 글의 내용을 생각하며 자세하게 다시 읽기
Step **2.** 빈칸을 채우며 문장 구조 생각하기

1 You can walk, run, stretch, and dance by moving your body. **2** Motor nerves allow the brain to control your muscles. **3** Thousands of muscles are attached to your bones. **4** When you want to move, your brain figures out which muscles are needed. **5** Then, the brain sends messages to these muscles, telling them to move your bones.

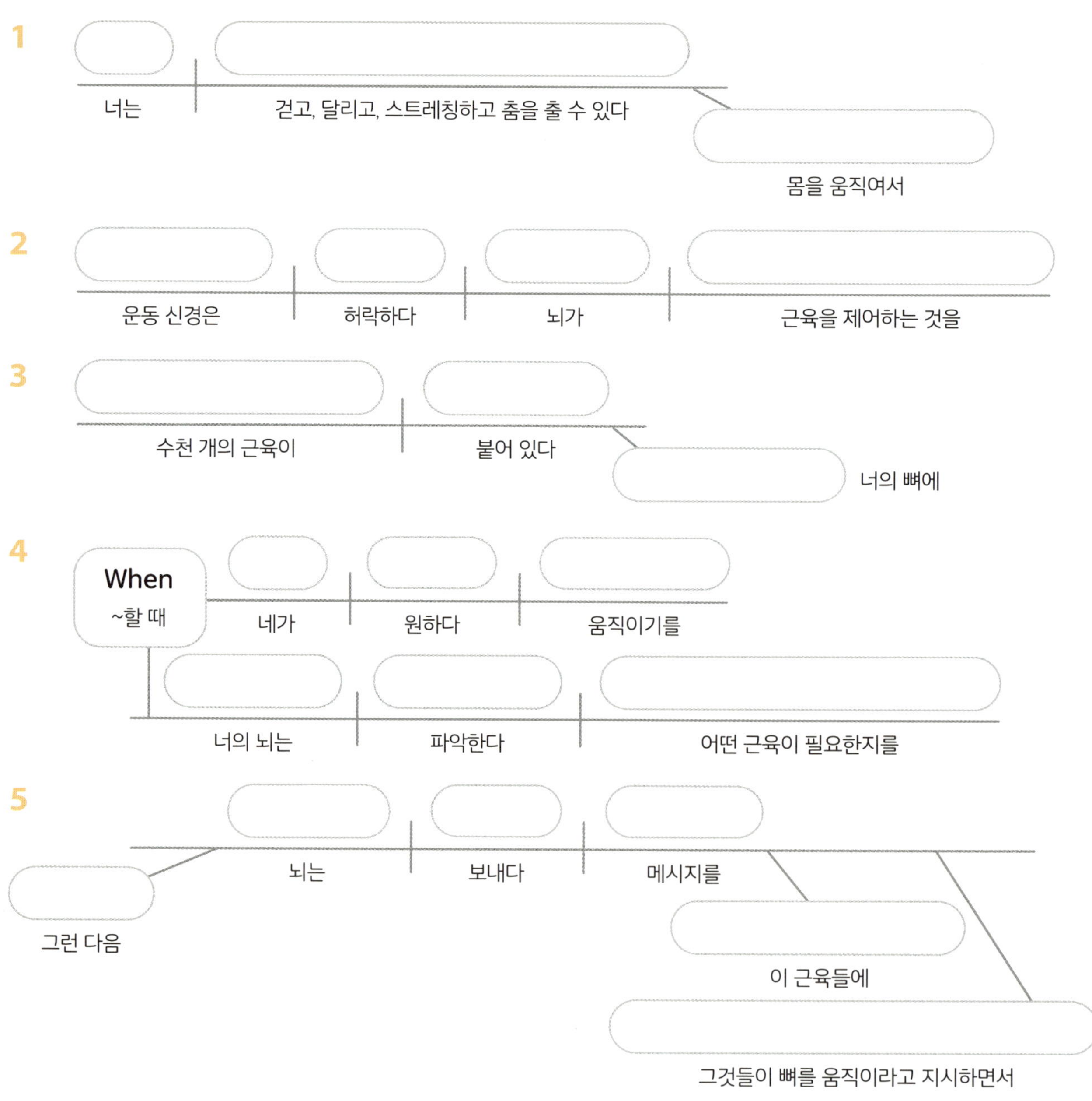

6 The human brain has more than 100 billion nerve cells. 7 The front part of the brain plans and makes decisions. 8 It does this by processing the different types of information received from nerve cells. 9 This information is called sensory information. 10 It comes from your senses, such as sight, hearing, touch, taste, and smell.

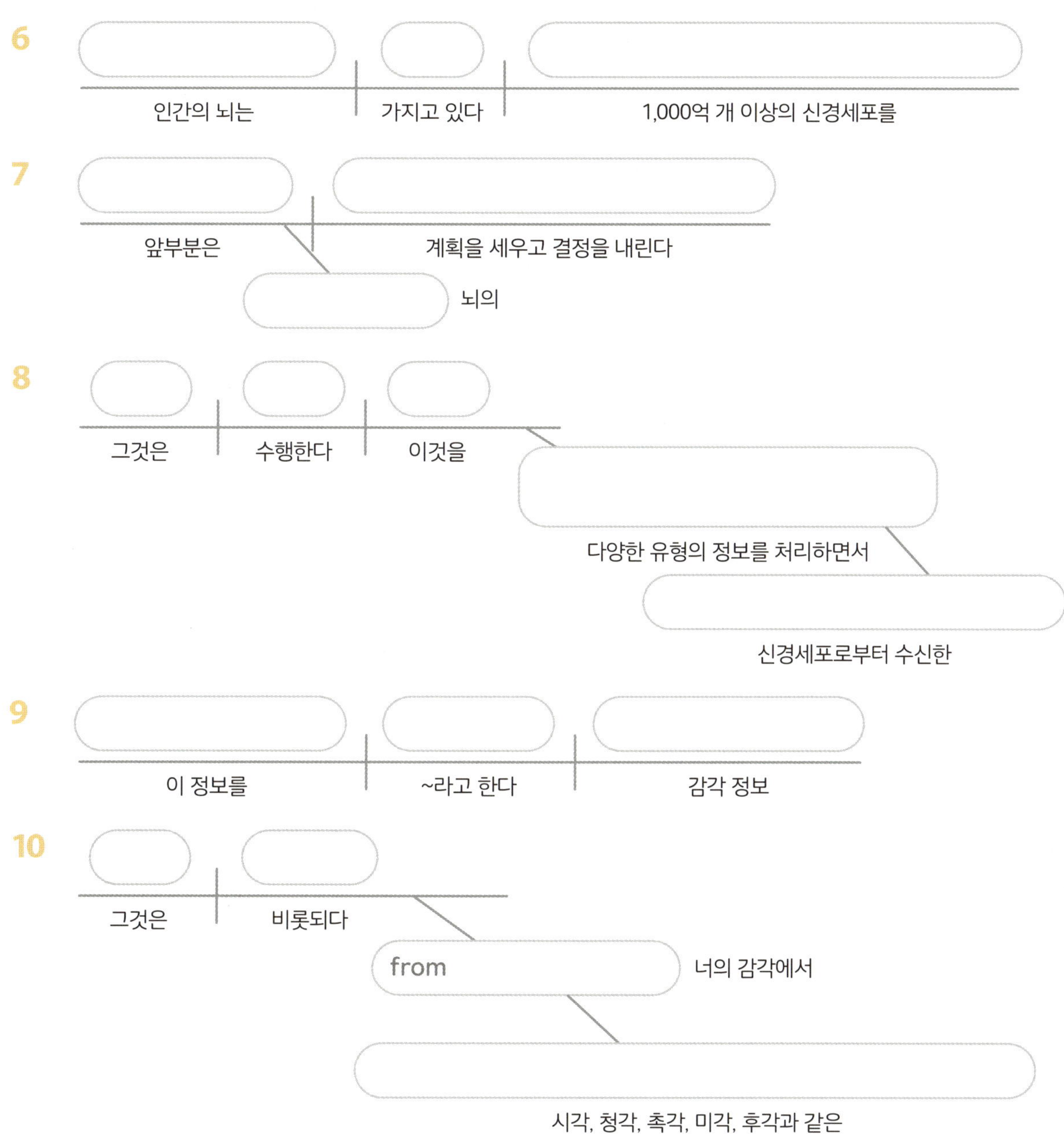

6 인간의 뇌는 | 가지고 있다 | 1,000억 개 이상의 신경세포를
7 앞부분은 | 계획을 세우고 결정을 내린다 | 뇌의
8 그것은 | 수행한다 | 이것을 | 다양한 유형의 정보를 처리하면서 | 신경세포로부터 수신한
9 이 정보를 | ~라고 한다 | 감각 정보
10 그것은 | 비롯되다 | from 너의 감각에서 | 시각, 청각, 촉각, 미각, 후각과 같은

Step **1.** 괄호에서 문장의 흐름에 알맞은 단어나 표현 고르기
Step **2.** 해석에 맞게 끊어 읽기(/) 표시하며 문장을 읽고, 빈칸에 알맞은 해석 쓰기

TIP 읽기 속도를 높이기 위해 짧은 <(접속사 +) 주어 + 동사>는 한 덩어리로 읽기

1 You can walk, (run, running), stretch, and dance by (move, moving) your body.
나열할 때는 같은 품사끼리   전치사 by + 명사 또는 동명사

→ 너는 걷고, / 달리고, 스트레칭하고, 춤을 출 수 있다 / ____________

2 Motor nerves (allows, allow) the brain (controls, to control) your muscles.
주어가 복수   allow + 목적어 + 목적 보어(to부정사)

→ 운동 신경은 허락한다 / 뇌가 / ____________

3 Thousands of muscles (is, are) attached *(in, to) your bones.
주어가 복수   be attached to: ~에 붙어 있다

→ ____________ / 붙어 있다 / 네 뼈에

4 When you want (to move, moving),
want + to부정사

→ 네가 원할 때 / 움직이기를 //

your brain (figure out, figures out) which muscles (is, are) needed.
주어가 단수   주어가 복수

→ 너의 뇌는 파악한다 / ____________

5 Then, the brain (send, sends) messages *(to, from) these muscles,
주어가 단수   send A to B

→ 그런 다음 / 뇌는 보낸다 / ____________ / 이 근육들에 //

telling them (move, to move) your bones.
tell + 목적어 + 목적 보어(to부정사)

→ 지시하면서 / 그것(근육)들에게 / ____________

6 The human brain (have, has) more (as, than) 100 billion nerve (cell, cells).
주어가 단수　　　　　～보다　　　　　billion + 복수명사

➜ 인간의 뇌는 가지고 있다 / ＿＿＿＿＿＿＿＿＿＿ 신경세포를

7 The front part of the brain (plan, plans) and (make, makes) decisions.
주어가 단수　　　and는 같은 역할 단어끼리 연결

➜ ＿＿＿＿＿＿＿＿＿ / 계획을 세우고 결정을 내린다

8 It (do, does) this by (process, processing) the different types of (information, informations)
주어가 단수　　　전치사 by + 명사 또는 동명사　　　셀 수 없는 명사

➜ 그것은 수행한다 / 이것을 / ＿＿＿＿＿＿＿＿＿＿ 처리하면서 //

received *(to, from) nerve (cell, cells).
～로부터　　　cell은 셀 수 있는 명사

➜ 신경 세포로부터 수신한

9 This information is (call, called) sensory information.
～라고 불리다

➜ 이 정보를 ~라고 한다 / ＿＿＿＿＿＿＿＿

10 It (come, comes) *from your senses, such as sight, (hear, hearing), touch, taste, and smell.
주어가 단수　　　나열할 때는 같은 품사끼리

➜ 이것은 비롯된다 / ＿＿＿＿＿＿ / 시각, 청각, 촉각, 미각, 후각과 같은

전치사 to와 from

전치사 to와 from은 둘 다 뒤에 시간이나 장소 표현을 쓸 수 있어요. 전치사 from은 '~로부터'라는 의미로 어떠한 일을 시작한 시점 또는 출발점, 어떤 일의 원인이나 유래, 출처를 의미하기도 해요.

- information received **from** nerve cells (receive from 받은 출처)
- It **comes from** your senses. (come from 유래, 출처)

반면에 전치사 to는 '~까지'라는 의미로 끝나는 시점 또는 도착점, 어떤 일의 결과나 방향을 나타내요.

- Thousands of muscles **are attached to** your bones. (attach to ~에)
- The brain **sends** messages **to** these muscles. (send A to B ~에게)

Unit 15

Preteens

A **Speed Reading** 빠르게 읽으며 내용상 중요 단어나 구라고 생각되는 부분에 동그라미 하세요.

Preteens are children between the ages of 9 and 12. This stage is the time of change between childhood and adolescence. Preteens usually experience significant physical and emotional changes, including the early stages of puberty. They pay more attention to how they look.

Preteens also experience social changes as they move toward becoming teenagers. They become more independent from their parents and spend more time with friends. They often form close friendships with peers of the same gender. Preteens may also become fascinated by famous athletes, musicians, or movie stars. They begin to explore their own identities, interests, and styles.

Words

preteen 사춘기 직전의 (아동) ｜ childhood 유년[아동]기 ｜ adolescence 청소년기 ｜ significant 중요한 ｜ physical 신체의
emotional 감정의 ｜ puberty 사춘기 ｜ pay attention to ~에 주목하다 ｜ independent 독립적인 ｜ peer 또래 ｜ gender 성별
fascinate 반하게 하다 ｜ athlete 운동선수 ｜ identity 정체, 동일성 ｜ interest 관심, 흥미

1   글의 내용과 일치하면 Yes, 틀리면 No에 동그라미 하세요.

1) Preteens are between childhood and adolescence.   Yes   No

2) Preteens experience significant physical changes.   Yes   No

3) Preteens are only interested in themselves.   Yes   No

2   글의 내용과 일치하도록 빈칸에 알맞은 단어를 써 보세요. (서술형)

Preteens are in the early stage of 1) p____________. They prefer to spend more time with friends than with their 2) p____________.

3   Preteen 시기에 겪는 중요한 3가지 변화를 우리말로 써 보세요. (서술형)

→ ____

C   **Checking Vocabulary**   단어를 영어로 바르게 설명한 것을 찾아 연결하세요.

1   adolescence •   • ⓐ   of the body

2   emotional •   • ⓑ   the period in a person's life between childhood and adulthood

3   physical •   • ⓒ   having to do with the feelings, including how one feels about oneself in relation to others

4   peer •   • ⓓ   a person who participates in sports or other physical activities

5   athlete •   • ⓔ   a person of the same rank, age group, or ability as another person

Step **1.** 글의 내용을 생각하며 자세하게 다시 읽기
Step **2.** 빈칸을 채우며 문장 구조 생각하기

1 Preteens are children between the ages of 9 and 12. **2** This stage is the time of change between childhood and adolescence. **3** Preteens usually experience significant physical and emotional changes, including the early stages of puberty. **4** They pay more attention to how they look.

5 Preteens also experience social changes as they move toward becoming teenagers. **6** They become more independent from their parents and spend more time with friends. **7** They often form close friendships with peers of the same gender. **8** Preteens may also become fascinated by famous athletes, musicians, or movie stars. **9** They begin to explore their own identities, interests, and styles.

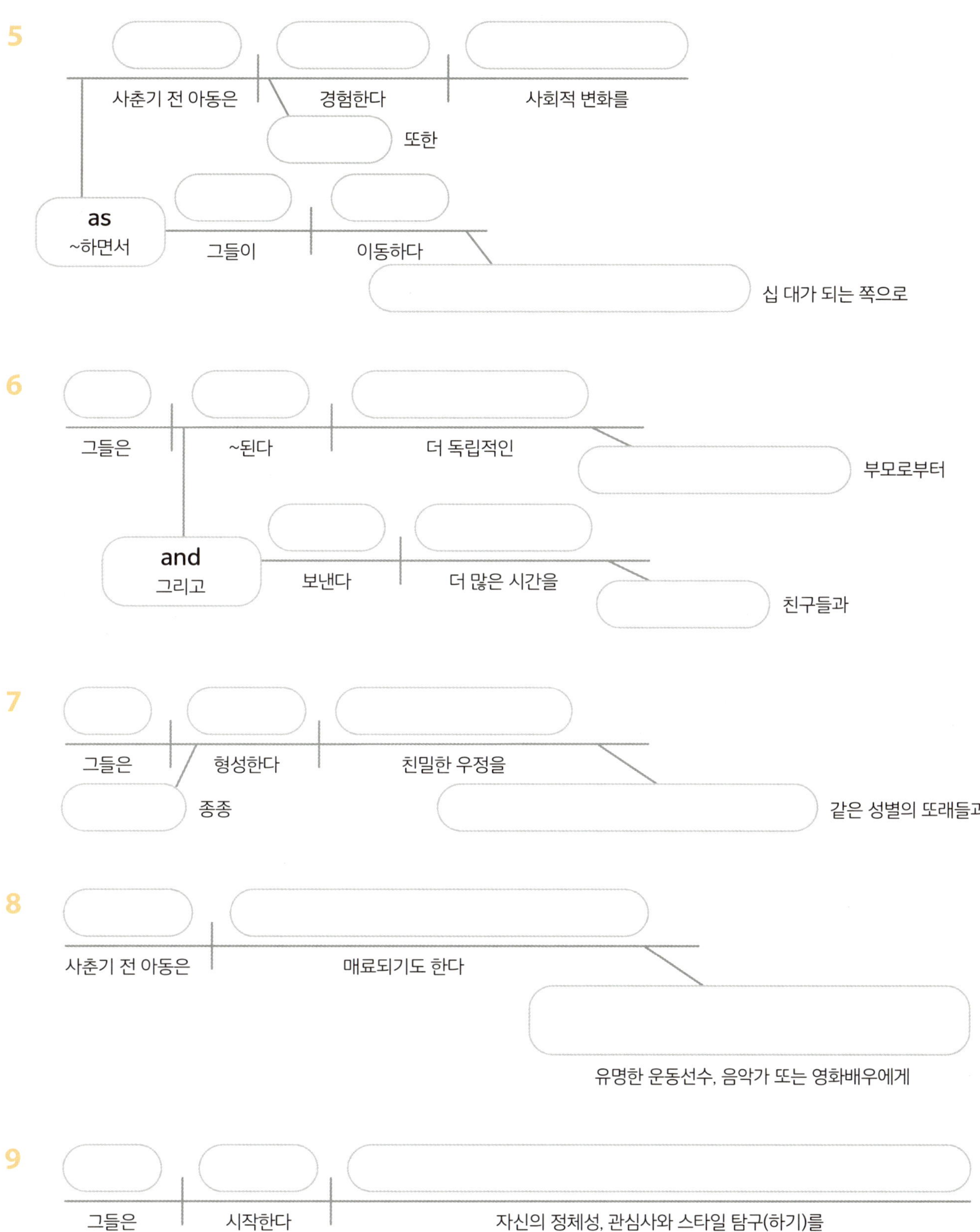

5
사춘기 전 아동은
경험한다
사회적 변화를
또한
as
~하면서
그들이
이동하다
십 대가 되는 쪽으로

6
그들은
~된다
더 독립적인
부모로부터
and
그리고
보낸다
더 많은 시간을
친구들과

7
그들은
형성한다
친밀한 우정을
종종
같은 성별의 또래들과

8
사춘기 전 아동은
매료되기도 한다
유명한 운동선수, 음악가 또는 영화배우에게

9
그들은
시작한다
자신의 정체성, 관심사와 스타일 탐구(하기)를

Step **1.** 괄호에서 문장의 흐름에 알맞은 단어나 표현 고르기
Step **2.** 해석에 맞게 끊어 읽기(/) 표시하며 문장을 읽고, 빈칸에 알맞은 해석 쓰기

TIP 읽기 속도를 높이기 위해 짧은 <(접속사 +) 주어 + 동사>는 한 덩어리로 읽기

1 Preteens (is, are) children between the ages of 9 (or, and) 12.
주어가 복수   between A and B: A와 B 사이

→ 사춘기 전 아동들은 ~이다 / 아이들 / ___________

2 (This, These) stage (is, are) the time of change between childhood and adolescence.
단수명사를 수식   주어가 단수

→ 이 시기는 ~이다 / 변화 시기 / ___________

3 Preteens (usually experience, experience usually) significant physical and emotional changes,
빈도부사 + 일반동사

→ 사춘기 전 아동들은 ___________ / 중요한 육체적, 정서적 변화를 //

(include, including) the early stages of puberty.
분사구문(~하면서)

→ ___________ 포함하면서

4 (He, They) pay more attention to (how, where) they look.
Preteens를 대신하는 대명사   동사 look의 보어

→ 그들은 기울인다 / ___________ / 자신이 어떻게 보일까에

5 Preteens also experience (socially, social) changes
명사를 수식하는 형용사

→ 사춘기 전 아동들은 또한 경험한다 / ___________ //

as they move (toward, from) becoming teenagers.
(어떤 방향을) 향하여

→ 그들이 이동하면서 / 십 대가 되는 쪽으로

6 They *(become, becoming) more independent (from, to) their parents
   동사가 올 자리   ~로부터

→ 그들은 된다 / 더 독립적으로 / ＿＿＿＿＿＿＿＿＿ //

and (spend, spends) more time with friends.
   they가 주어

→ 그리고 보낸다 / ＿＿＿＿＿＿＿＿＿ / 친구들과

7 They (often form, form often) close friendships (for, with) peers of the same gender.
   빈도부사 + 일반동사   ~와

→ 그들은 종종 형성한다 / 친밀한 우정을 / ＿＿＿＿＿＿＿＿＿

8 Preteens may also *(become, becomes) fascinated
   조동사 + 동사원형

→ 사춘기 전 아동들은 / 또한 매료될 수 있다 //

(by, at) famous athletes, musicians, or movie stars.
~에 의해(수동)

→ ＿＿＿＿＿＿＿＿＿, 또는 영화배우에게

9 They begin (explore, to explore) their own identities, interests, and styles.
   begin + to 부정사

→ 그들은 시작한다 / 자신의 ＿＿＿＿＿＿＿＿＿ 탐구하기를

동사 become/get/grow/turn + 보어
주어가 '~하게 되다'라는 상태 변화를 의미하는 동사 become, get, grow, turn 뒤에는 형용사 보어를 써요.

- They **become** more independent from their parents.
- Preteens may **become** fascinated by famous athletes.
- He **got** tired. 그는 피곤해졌다.
- The sky **grew** dark. 하늘이 어두워졌다.
- The leaves were **turning** brown. 나뭇잎들이 누렇게 변하고 있었다.
- She **became** wiser as she **grew** older. 그녀는 나이를 먹음에 따라 더 현명해졌다.

Unit 16 — Sickness

A Speed Reading

빠르게 읽으며 내용상 중요 단어나 구라고 생각되는 부분에 동그라미 하세요.

Sickness is the feeling that occurs when your body or mind isn't working as well as usual. It can happen for many reasons. Often, sickness is caused by tiny living things called germs. Some illnesses are inherited from parents. Others are caused by pollution, chemicals, or radiation. Depression or anxiety can affect your mind.

Your body fights off germs by sending special cells to attack them. Billions of germs live on the outside of your body all the time. Most are harmless, but some can cause illnesses like colds, the flu, or measles. Other germs can make parts of your body hurt. Keeping your body clean helps you stay healthy.

Words

sickness 질병 | occur 발생하다 | germ 세균, 미생물 | reason 이유 | illness 병, 아픔 | pollution 오염, 공해 | chemical 화학 물질
radiation 방사능 | depression 우울증 | anxiety 불안 | affect ~에 영향을 미치다 | fight off 싸워서 격퇴하다 | attack 공격하다 | billions of 수십억의
harmless 무해한 | measles 홍역

B **Reading for Information** 글을 빠르게 다시 읽고, 아래 질문에 답하세요.

1 글의 내용과 일치하면 Yes, 틀리면 No에 동그라미 하세요.

1) Sickness can be caused by many reasons.   **Yes**   **No**

2) All the germs are harmful.   **Yes**   **No**

3) Some illnesses are inherited from parents.   **Yes**   **No**

2 글의 내용과 일치하도록 빈칸에 알맞은 단어를 써 보세요. (서술형)

G__________ are tiny living things that can be found on the outside of your body. While most of them are harmless, some can cause sickness.

3 세균으로 인한 질병을 예방하는 방법을 우리말로 써 보세요. (서술형)

→

C **Checking Vocabulary** 단어를 영어로 바르게 설명한 것을 찾아 연결하세요.

1 sickness ●   ● ⓐ something that makes the Earth dirty

2 pollution ●   ● ⓑ unhealthy condition of body or mind

3 depression ●   ● ⓒ to hurt or destroy; to begin to cause harm to

4 attack ●   ● ⓓ lacking the power or intention to cause harm

5 harmless ●   ● ⓔ deep sadness or low spirits

Step **1.** 글의 내용을 생각하며 자세하게 다시 읽기
Step **2.** 빈칸을 채우며 문장 구조 생각하기

1 Sickness is the feeling that occurs when your body or mind isn't working as well as usual. **2** It can happen for many reasons. **3** Often, sickness is caused by tiny living things called germs. **4** Some illnesses are inherited from parents. **5** Others are caused by pollution, chemicals, or radiation. **6** Depression or anxiety can affect your mind.

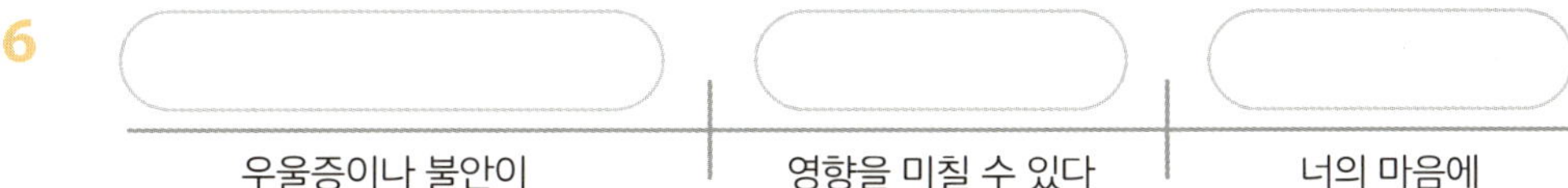

6

우울증이나 불안이 | 영향을 미칠 수 있다 | 너의 마음에

7 Your body fights off germs by sending special cells to attack them. **8** Billions of germs live on the outside of your body all the time. **9** Most are harmless, but some can cause illnesses like colds, the flu, or measles. **10** Other germs can make parts of your body hurt. **11** Keeping your body clean helps you stay healthy.

7

네 몸은 | 물리친다 | 세균을

특수 세포를 보내서   그것(세균)들을 공격하기 위해

8

수십억 마리의 세균이 | 살고 있다

몸 바깥에   항상

9

대부분은 | ~이다 | 무해한

but 그러나

어떤 것들은 | 일으킬 수 있다 | 질병을

감기, 독감이나 홍역과 같은

10

다른 세균들은 | 만들 수 있다 | 네 신체 일부를 | 아프게

11

몸을 청결하게 유지하는 것은 | 도움을 준다 | 네가 | 건강을 유지하는 데

Step **1.** 괄호에서 문장의 흐름에 알맞은 단어나 표현 고르기
Step **2.** 해석에 맞게 끊어 읽기(/) 표시하며 문장을 읽고, 빈칸에 알맞은 해석 쓰기

🔖 **TIP** 읽기 속도를 높이기 위해 짧은 <(접속사 +) 주어 + 동사>는 한 덩어리로 읽기

1 Sickness (is, are) the feeling that (occur, occurs)
        셀 수 없는 명사 주어는 단수 취급   that의 선행사 feeling이 단수

→ 질병은 ~이다 / 감각 / _____________ //

when your body or mind isn't (working, work) as well (as, than) usual.
        진행형: be동사 + 동사-ing   동급비교: as ~ as

→ ~할 때 / 몸이나 마음이 / _____________ / 평소만큼 잘

2 It can (happen, happens) for many (reason, reasons).
        조동사 + 동사원형   many + 복수명사

→ 그것은 발생할 수 있다 / _____________

3 Often, sickness is (caused, causes) by tiny living things (calling, called) germs.
        수동태: be동사 + 과거분사(p.p.)   ~라고 불리는

→ 종종 / 질병은 발생한다 / _____________ / 세균이라고 하는

4 *Some illnesses (is, are) inherited (to, from) parents.
        주어가 복수   ~로부터

→ 일부 질병들은 / _____________ / 부모로부터

5 *Others are (causing, caused) by pollution, chemicals, or radiation.
        수동태: be동사 + 과거분사(p.p.)

→ 다른 질병들은 발생한다 / 오염, 화학물질 또는 _____________

6 Depression or (anxious, anxiety) can affect your mind.
        명사가 주어 역할

→ _____________ / 영향을 미칠 수 있다 / 너의 마음에

7 Your body fights off germs by (send, sending) special cells to (attack, attacking) them.
전치사 by + 명사나 동명사　　　　　　　to 부정사 : ~하기 위해서

→ 네 몸은 물리친다 / 세균을 / 특수 세포를 보내 / ＿＿＿＿＿＿＿＿

8 Billions of (germ, germs) live on the outside of your body all the (time, times).
billions of + 복수명사　　　　　　　time은 셀 수 없는 명사

→ 수십억 마리의 세균이 / 살고 있다 / 너의 몸 바깥에 / ＿＿＿＿＿＿＿＿

9 *Most (is, are) harmless,
most 뒤에 of germs가 생략된 복수 주어

→ 대부분은 ~이다 / 무해한 //

but *some can cause (ill, illnesses) like colds, the flu, or measles.
명사가 목적어 역할

→ 그러나 일부는 일으킬 수 있다 / 질병을 / ＿＿＿＿＿＿＿＿

10 * (Another, Other) germs can make parts of your body (to hurt, hurt).
복수명사 germs와 함께 쓸 수 있는 것　　　　　　　make + 목적어 + 목적 보어(동사원형)

→ 다른 세균들은 / 만들 수 있다 / ＿＿＿＿＿＿＿＿ / 아프게

11 (Keep, Keeping) your body clean (help, helps) you stay healthy.
주어 역할의 동명사　　　　　　　동명사 주어는 단수 취급

→ 몸을 청결하게 유지하는 것은 / 도움을 준다 / 네가 / ＿＿＿＿＿＿＿＿

most, some, other

most, some, other는 뒤에 바로 복수명사나 셀 수 없는 명사를 쓰거나, 홀로 대명사처럼 쓸 수 있어요.

- **Some** illnesses are inherited from parents. (형용사: 몇몇)
- **Others** are caused by pollution, chemicals, or radiation. (대명사: 다른 것들)
- **Most** are harmless, but **some** can cause illnesses. (대명사: 대부분 / 몇몇)
- **Other** germs can make parts of your body hurt. (형용사: 다른)

Spiders

Unit 17_mp3

A **Speed Reading** 빠르게 읽으며 내용상 중요 단어나 구라고 생각되는 부분에 동그라미 하세요.

Spiders are not insects. They have eight legs instead of six. They come in many shapes and colors. They have special eyes to see in the dark and tiny hairs on their legs to sense their surroundings. Most spiders are harmless to humans and help control pests by eating them.

While most spiders eat insects, some feed on frogs, fish, and small animals. All spiders spin sticky silk threads. The silk acts as a safety rope, helping them climb or escape danger. Spiders also use silk to build webs for catching and wrapping prey. They make nests and protect their eggs.

Words

sense 감지하다 ㅣ surroundings 환경 ㅣ pest 해충 ㅣ feed on ~을 먹고 살다 ㅣ spin (거미·누에가) 실을 내다, 돌리다 ㅣ sticky 끈적끈적한
thread 실, 가닥 ㅣ safety 안전 ㅣ escape 벗어나다 ㅣ web 거미줄, 망 ㅣ wrap 싸다 ㅣ prey 먹이, 사냥감

B **Reading for Information** 글을 빠르게 다시 읽고, 아래 질문에 답하세요.

1 글의 내용과 일치하면 Yes, 틀리면 No에 동그라미 하세요.

1) Spiders and insects have six legs. **Yes** **No**

2) Most spiders are harmful to humans. **Yes** **No**

3) Some spiders feed on small animals. **Yes** **No**

2 글의 내용과 일치하도록 빈칸에 알맞은 단어를 써 보세요. (서술형)

Spiders are not insects. Insects have 1) s__________ legs but spiders have 2) e__________ legs. All spiders spin sticky 3) s__________ threads.

3 거미가 사람들에게 도움이 되는 부분을 우리말로 써 보세요. (서술형)

→ ~~~~~~

C **Checking Vocabulary** 단어를 영어로 바르게 설명한 것을 찾아 연결하세요.

1 prey • • ⓐ an insect or animal that causes damage to crops, or is harmful

2 sense • • ⓑ something a spider makes to catch bugs

3 pest • • ⓒ an animal that is eaten by another animal

4 escape • • ⓓ to feel or experience using your senses

5 web • • ⓔ to get away, to get free; to avoid being caught or harmed

Step **1.** 글의 내용을 생각하며 자세하게 다시 읽기
Step **2.** 빈칸을 채우며 문장 구조 생각하기

1 Spiders are not insects. **2** They have eight legs instead of six. **3** They come in many shapes and colors. **4** They have special eyes to see in the dark and tiny hairs on their legs to sense their surroundings. **5** Most spiders are harmless to humans and help control pests by eating them.

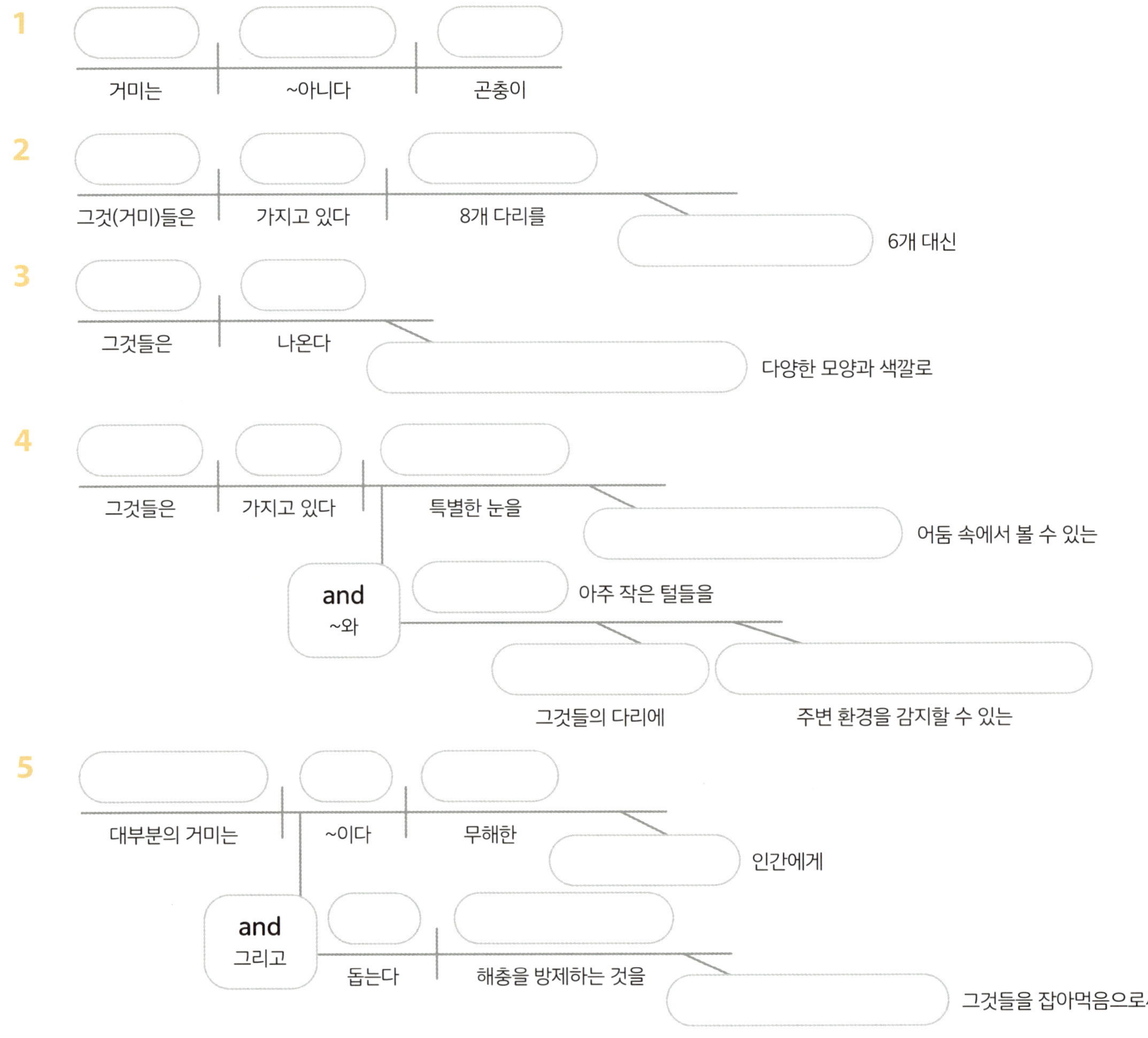

6 While most spiders eat insects, some feed on frogs, fish, and small animals. **7** All spiders spin sticky silk threads. **8** The silk acts as a safety rope, helping them climb or escape danger. **9** Spiders also use silk to build webs for catching and wrapping prey. **10** They make nests and protect their eggs.

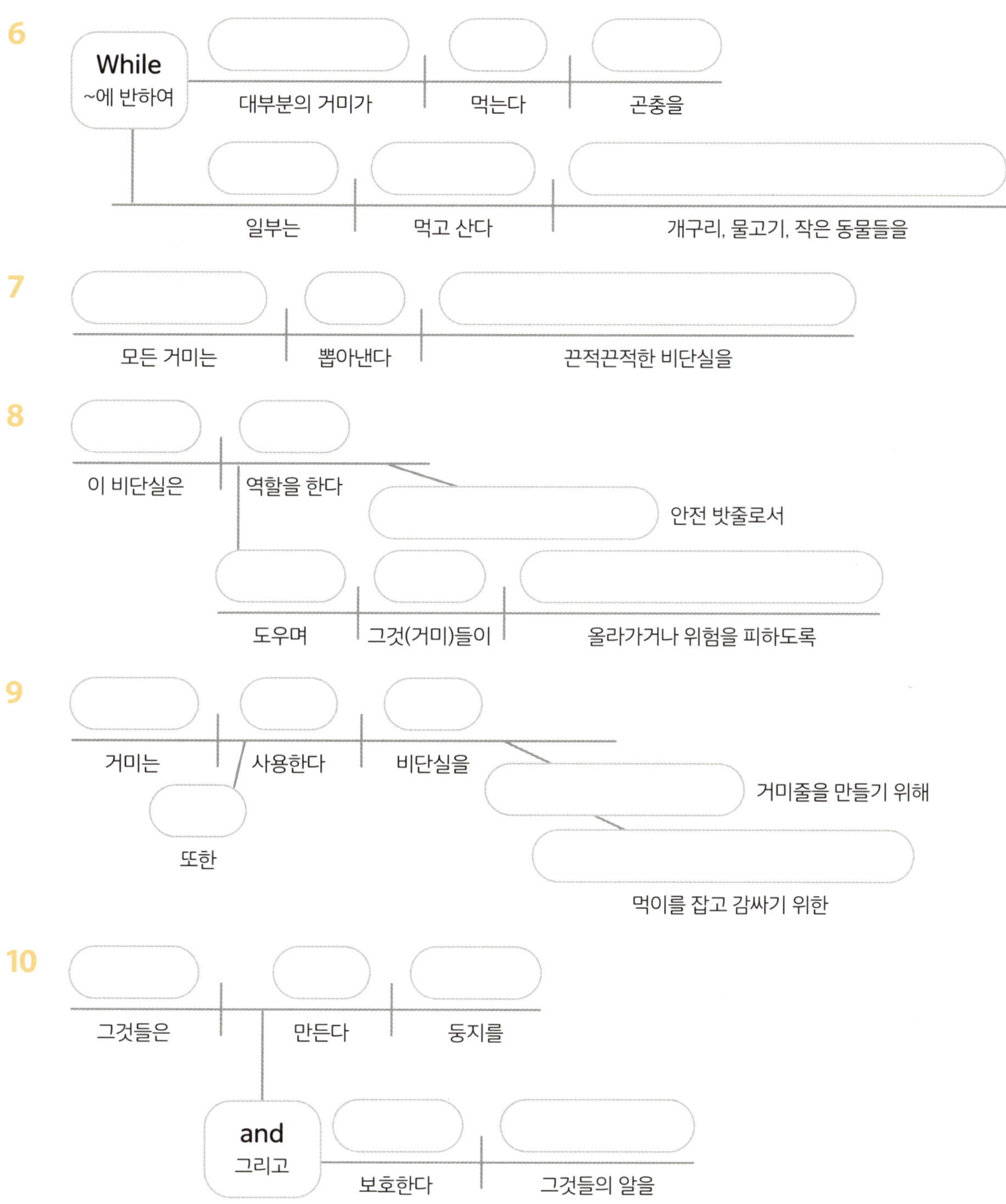

Step **1.** 괄호에서 문장의 흐름에 알맞은 단어나 표현 고르기
Step **2.** 해석에 맞게 끊어 읽기(/) 표시하며 문장을 읽고, 빈칸에 알맞은 해석 쓰기

💠 **TIP** 읽기 속도를 높이기 위해 짧은 <(접속사 +) 주어 + 동사>는 한 덩어리로 읽기

1   Spiders (is, are) not insects.
　　　　주어가 복수

→ 거미는 ~ 아니다 / ＿＿＿＿＿＿＿＿

2   (It, They) have eight (leg, legs) instead of six.
　　앞의 주어 Spiders를 대신　　　eight 뒤에는 복수 명사

→ 그것들은 가지고 있다 / ＿＿＿＿＿＿＿＿ / 6개가 아니라

3   They (come, comes) in (much, many) shapes and colors.
　　　　　주어가 복수　　　　셀 수 있는 명사 앞

→ 그것들은 나온다 / ＿＿＿＿＿＿＿＿ 색깔로

4   They have special eyes (to see, seeing) in the dark
　　　　　　　　명사 eyes를 수식하는 형용사 역할

→ 그것들은 가지고 있다 / 특별한 눈을 / ＿＿＿＿＿＿＿＿ 볼 수 있는 //

and tiny hairs (on, in) their legs (to sense, sensing) their surroundings.
　　　　　　다리 표면에 붙은 상태　　　명사 legs를 수식하는 형용사 역할

→ 그리고 아주 작은 털들을 / ＿＿＿＿＿＿＿＿ / 그들의 주변 환경을 감지할 수 있는

5   Most (spider, spiders) are harmless to humans
　　　　most + 셀 수 있는 명사 복수

→ 대부분의 거미는 ~이다/ 무해한 / ＿＿＿＿＿＿＿＿ //

and (help, helps) control pests *by (eat, eating) them.
　　　　주어가 복수　　　　　　　　　전치사 + 동명사

→ 그리고 돕는다 / 해충을 방제하는 것을 / ＿＿＿＿＿＿＿＿

6 (While, As) most spiders (eat, eats) insects,
'대조'를 나타내는 접속사   주어가 복수

➜ 대부분의 거미가 먹는 데 반해 / 곤충을 //

some (feed on, feeds on) frogs, (fish, fishes), and small animals.
주어가 복수   단·복수 모양이 같음

➜ ＿＿＿＿＿＿＿＿ / 개구리, 물고기와 작은 동물들을

7 All (spiders, spider) spin sticky silk threads.
all + 셀 수 있는 명사 복수형

➜ ＿＿＿＿＿＿＿＿ / 끈적한 비단실을

8 The silk (acts, act) as a safety rope, helping (they, them) climb or escape danger.
주어가 단수   help + 목적어+ 목적 보어

➜ 그 비단실은 역할을 한다 / ＿＿＿＿＿＿ / 도우며 / 그것들이 / 올라가거나 위험을 피하도록

9 Spiders also use silk (building, to build) webs *for (to catch, catching) and wrapping prey.
~하기 위해서(목적)   전치사 for + 동명사

➜ 거미는 또한 사용한다 / 비단실을 / 거미줄을 만들기 위해 / ＿＿＿＿＿＿＿

10 They make nests and (protect, protects) their eggs.
주어가 they

➜ 그것들은 만든다 / ＿＿＿＿＿＿ / 그리고 보호한다 / (그것들의) 알을

Unit 18 — Teens

A **Speed Reading** 빠르게 읽으며 내용상 중요 단어나 구라고 생각되는 부분에 동그라미 하세요.

Teenagers are no longer children. During puberty, they experience rapid physical growth and changes. Becoming a teenager is like getting a new body. Looking good becomes important to most teens. Friendships and peer relationships also become more important. This stage is full of growth and discovery.

Teenagers are eager to learn about the world. For the first time, they can do things on their own without any adults around. They may test boundaries and seek new experiences. As they develop advanced thinking skills, they explore their identity. Strong emotions and mood swings are common as they navigate these changes.

Words

teen 십 대 (= teenager) ㅣ rapid 빠른 ㅣ relationship 관계 ㅣ discovery 발견 ㅣ eager 열심인, 열렬한 ㅣ boundary 경계 ㅣ seek 찾다, 추구하다
advanced 상급의 ㅣ mood swing 기분 변화, 감정 기복 ㅣ common 흔한 ㅣ navigate (복잡한 상황을) 다루다, 탐색하다 ㅣ appearance 외모

B **Reading for Information** 글을 빠르게 다시 읽고, 아래 질문에 답하세요.

1 글의 내용과 일치하면 Yes, 틀리면 No에 동그라미 하세요.

1) Teenagers are still children. **Yes** **No**

2) Teenagers experience rapid changes. **Yes** **No**

3) Teens are interested in their appearance. **Yes** **No**

2 글의 내용과 일치하도록 빈칸에 알맞은 단어를 써 보세요. (서술형)

Becoming a teenager is like getting a new 1) b___________ because they experience rapid 2) p___________ growth and changes during puberty.

3 십 대 사춘기 단계에 흔히 나타나는 정서적인 특징을 우리말로 써 보세요. (서술형)

➡

C **Checking Vocabulary** 단어를 영어로 바르게 설명한 것을 찾아 연결하세요.

1 rapid • • ⓐ the way people or things are connected to each other

2 relationship • • ⓑ happening in a short or brief time; moving quickly

3 eager • • ⓒ a person's feelings change quickly

4 boundary • • ⓓ very excited and interested in doing something; wanting very much

5 mood swing • • ⓔ a line or limit that separates two things or areas

D　Reading for Learning

Step **1.** 글의 내용을 생각하며 자세하게 다시 읽기
Step **2.** 빈칸을 채우며 문장 구조 생각하기

1 Teenagers are no longer children. **2** During puberty, they experience rapid physical growth and changes. **3** Becoming a teenager is like getting a new body. **4** Looking good becomes important to most teens. **5** Friendships and peer relationships also become more important. **6** This stage is full of growth and discovery.

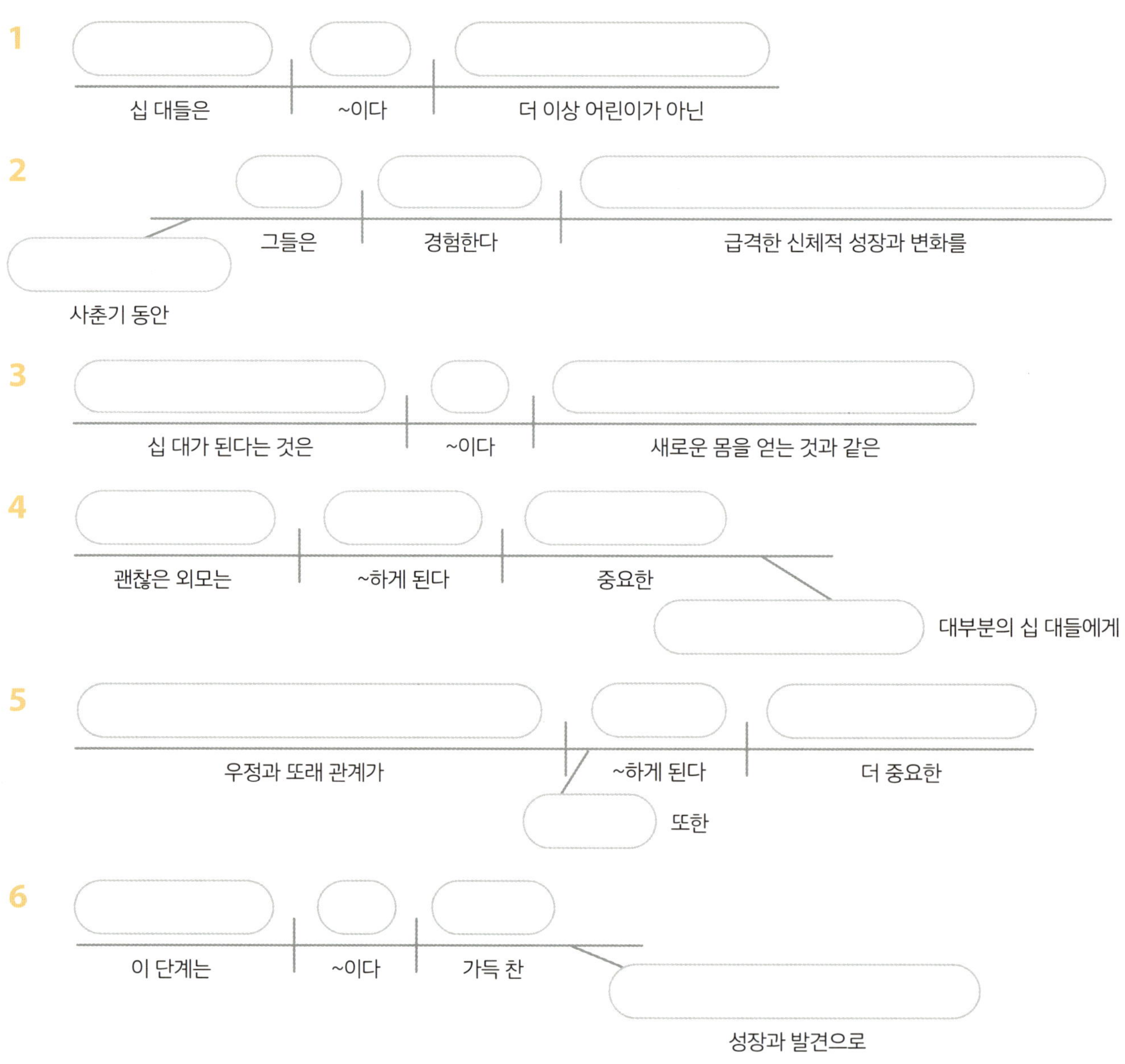

7 Teenagers are eager to learn about the world. **8** For the first time, they can do things on their own without any adults around. **9** They may test boundaries and seek new experiences. **10** As they develop advanced thinking skills, they explore their identity. **11** Strong emotions and mood swings are common as they navigate these changes.

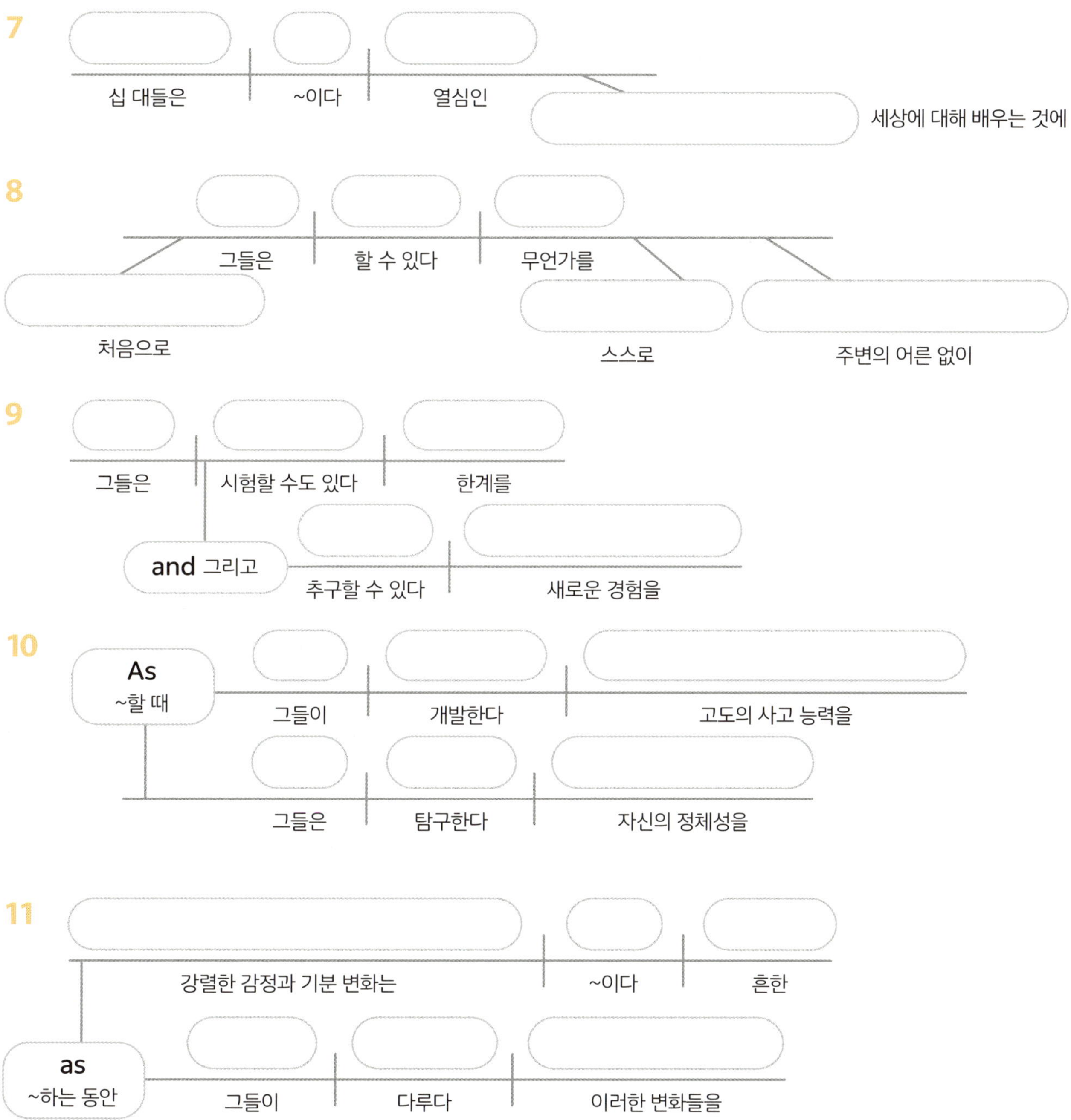

Step **1.** 괄호에서 문장의 흐름에 알맞은 단어나 표현 고르기
Step **2.** 해석에 맞게 끊어 읽기(/) 표시하며 문장을 읽고, 빈칸에 알맞은 해석 쓰기

> 🔧 TIP 읽기 속도를 높이기 위해 짧은 <(접속사 +) 주어 + 동사>는 한 덩어리로 읽기

1   Teenagers are no longer (childs, children).
         child의 복수형은 불규칙

→ 십 대들은 ~이다 / ___________________

2   (For, During) puberty, they experience rapid physical (grow, growth) and changes.
         특정 기간과 함께 쓰는 전치사   목적어로 쓰는 명사형

→ ___________ / 그들은 경험한다 / 급격한 신체적 성장과 변화를

3   *(Become, Becoming) a teenager is like (get, getting) a new body.
              주어 역할을 하는 동명사   전치사 like + 동명사

→ 십 대가 된다는 것은 ~이다 / ___________________ 같은

4   *(Look, Looking) good (become, becomes) important to most teens.
              주어 역할을 하는 동명사   동명사는 단수 취급

→ 괜찮은 외모는 ~해진다 / 중요한 / ___________________

5   Friendships and peer relationships also (become, becomes) more important.
                                          and로 연결된 주어는 복수 취급

→ 우정과 또래 관계는 / 또한 ~해진다 / ___________________

6   This stage is full (of, with) growth and (discover, discovery).
                   be full of: ~로 가득 차다   and는 같은 품사 단어끼리 연결

→ 이 단계는 ~이다 / 가득 찬 / ___________________으로

7   Teenagers are eager (learning, to learn) about the world.
                          be eager + to 부정사

→ 십 대들은 ~이다 / 열심인 / ___________________ 배우는 것에

8 For the first (time, times), they can do things on their own (with, without) any adults around.
　　time은 셀 수 없는 명사　　　　　　　　　　　　　　　　　　　　　　　　~없이

→ ＿＿＿＿＿＿ / 그들은 할 수 있다 / 무언가를 / 스스로 / 주변의 어른 없이

9 They (must, may) test boundaries and (seek, to seek) new experiences.
　　~할지도 모른다(가능)　　　　　　　　and는 같은 품사 단어끼리 연결

→ 그들은 ＿＿＿＿＿＿ / 한계를 / 그리고 추구할 수 있다 / 새로운 경험을

10 As (he, they) develop advanced thinking skills,
　　앞 문장의 주어와 동일한 인칭대명사

→ 그들이 개발하면서 / 고도의 사고 능력을 //

they (explore, explores) their identity.
　　　　　　주어가 복수

→ 그들은 탐색한다 / ＿＿＿＿＿＿

11 Strong emotions and mood swings (is, are) common
　　　　　　　　　　　and로 연결된 주어는 복수 취급

→ ＿＿＿＿＿＿ / ~이다 / 흔한 //

as they navigate (this, these) changes.
　　　　　　복수명사를 수식

→ 그들이 탐색하는 동안 / ＿＿＿＿＿＿

동명사

동명사(동사-ing)는 문장에서 주어, 목적어, 보어 역할을 해요.
동명사가 주어로 쓰일 땐 단수 취급을 하고, 동명사 뒤에는 보어나 목적어를 쓸 수 있어요.

- **Becoming** a teenager **is** like getting a new body.
　동명사 주어　　　　단수동사

- **Looking** good **becomes** important to most teens.
　동명사 주어　　　　단수동사

Unit 19

Volcanoes

A **Speed Reading** 빠르게 읽으며 내용상 중요 단어나 구라고 생각되는 부분에 동그라미 하세요.

The ground under your feet seems solid, but in some places, it is weak or cracked. These weak spots are where volcanoes form. A volcano is an opening in the Earth's crust. Through this opening, melted rock, ash, and gases are expelled. The melted rock beneath the Earth's crust is called magma. When it flows out of a volcano, it is called lava.

Lava can sometimes move very fast, like a red-hot river. Volcanoes are often cone-shaped mountains, formed from hardened lava. However, they come in many shapes and sizes and are found all over the world. Volcanic eruptions play a key role in shaping the Earth's landscape.

Words

solid 단단한 ┃ cracked 갈라진 ┃ spot 지점 ┃ volcano 화산 (volcanic 화산의) ┃ opening 구멍, 틈 ┃ crust 딱딱한 표면, 껍질 ┃ melted 녹은
ash 재 ┃ expel 배출하다 ┃ beneath ~아래 ┃ magma 마그마 ┃ lava 용암 ┃ cone-shaped 원뿔 모양의 ┃ hardened 굳어진 ┃ eruption 분출
play a key role 핵심적인 역할을 하다 ┃ landscape 풍경, 지형

1 글의 내용과 일치하면 Yes, 틀리면 No에 동그라미 하세요.

1) The ground under your feet is always solid. **Yes** **No**

2) Volcanoes are often formed from hardened lava. **Yes** **No**

3) Volcanoes are found only in certain parts of the world. **Yes** **No**

2 글의 내용과 일치하도록 빈칸에 알맞은 단어를 써 보세요. (서술형)

1) M___________ is the melted rock beneath the Earth's crust. When magma flows out of a volcano, it is called 2) l___________.

3 화산이라는 구멍 밖으로 배출되는 3가지를 찾아 우리말로 써 보세요. (서술형)

➔ ____

C **C**hecking Vocabulary 단어를 영어로 바르게 설명한 것을 찾아 연결하세요.

1 solid •   • ⓐ the hot, melted rock that comes out of a volcano

2 lava •   • ⓑ to change from a solid to a liquid because of heat, like ice turning into water

3 melt •   • ⓒ to force something or someone to leave a place

4 hardened •   • ⓓ having a firm shape; not like a liquid or a gas

5 expel •   • ⓔ having become hard or firm

Step **1.** 글의 내용을 생각하며 자세하게 다시 읽기
Step **2.** 빈칸을 채우며 문장 구조 생각하기

1 The ground under your feet seems solid, but in some places, it is weak or cracked. **2** These weak spots are where volcanoes form. **3** A volcano is an opening in the Earth's crust. **4** Through this opening, melted rock, ash, and gases are expelled. **5** The melted rock beneath the Earth's crust is called magma. **6** When it flows out of a volcano, it is called lava.

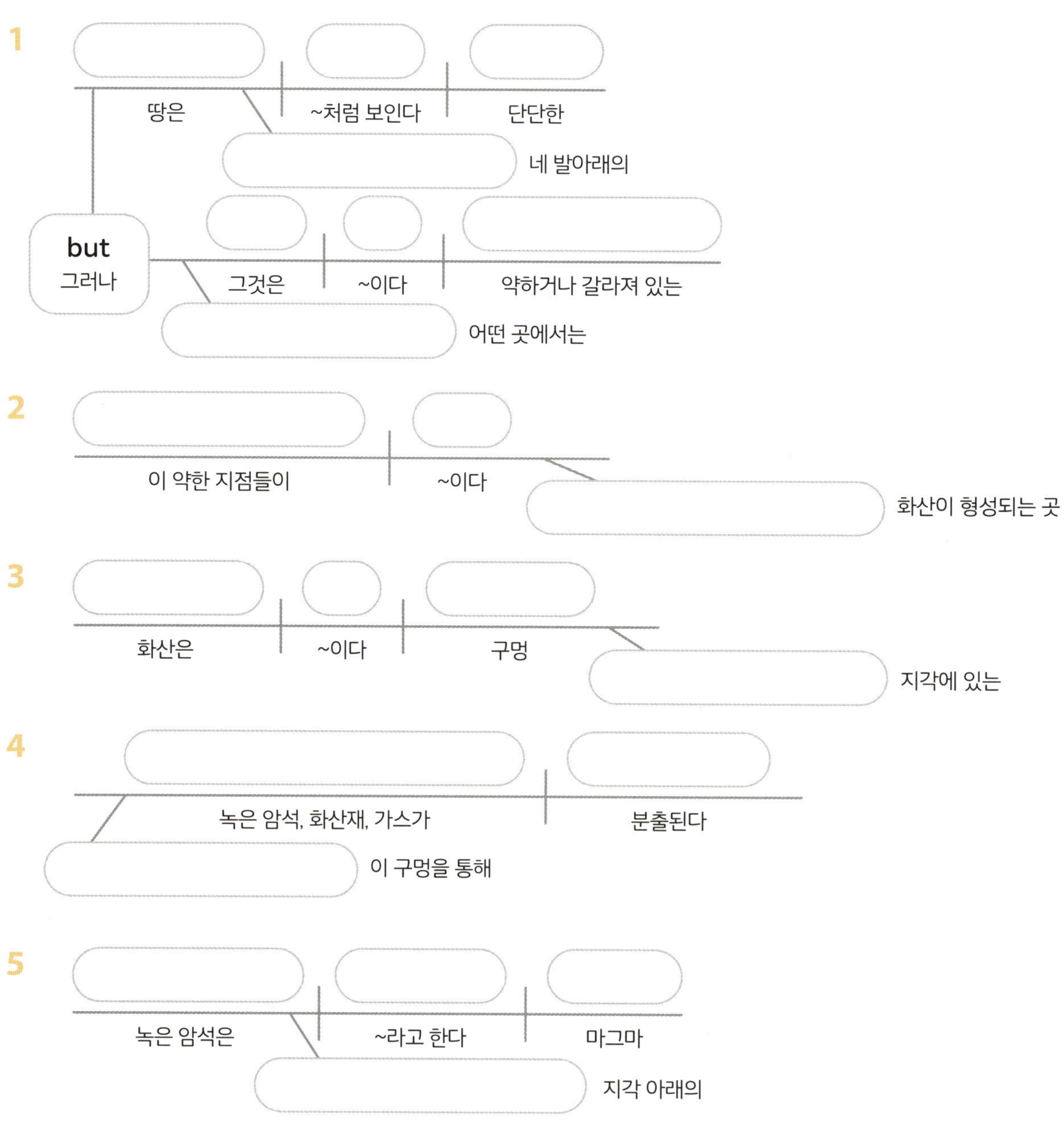

6

When
~할 때

그것이 흐른다 화산 밖으로

그것은 불린다 용암

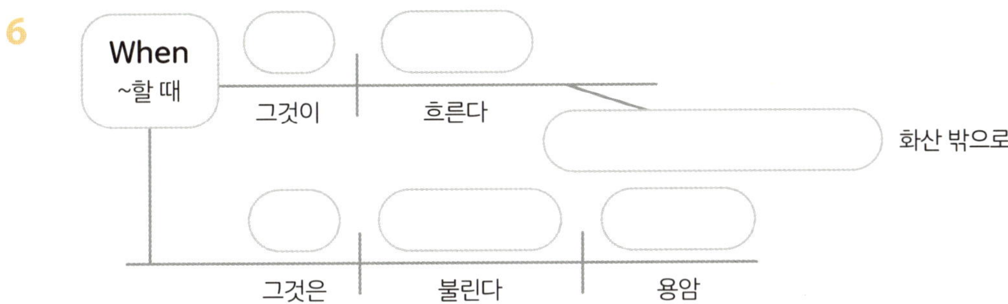

7 Lava can sometimes move very fast, like a red-hot river. **8** Volcanoes are often cone-shaped mountains, formed from hardened lava. **9** However, they come in many shapes and sizes and are found all over the world. **10** Volcanic eruptions play a key role in shaping the Earth's landscape.

7

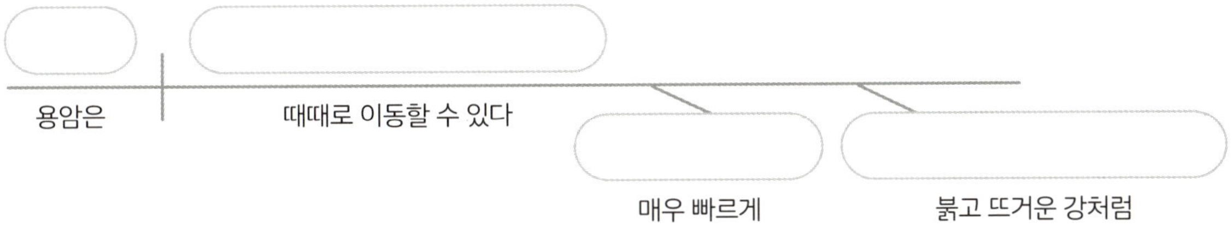

용암은 때때로 이동할 수 있다

매우 빠르게 붉고 뜨거운 강처럼

8

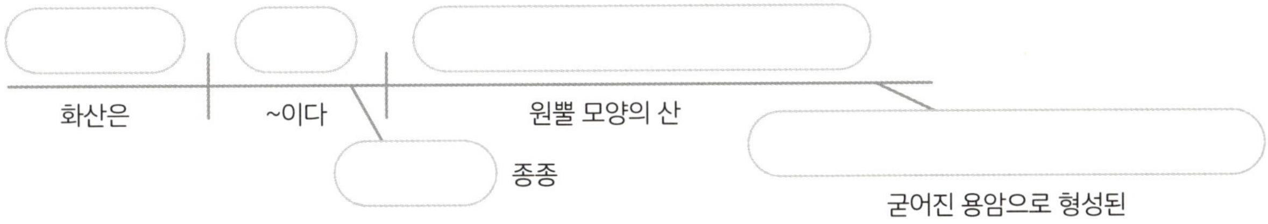

화산은 ~이다 원뿔 모양의 산

종종 굳어진 용암으로 형성된

9

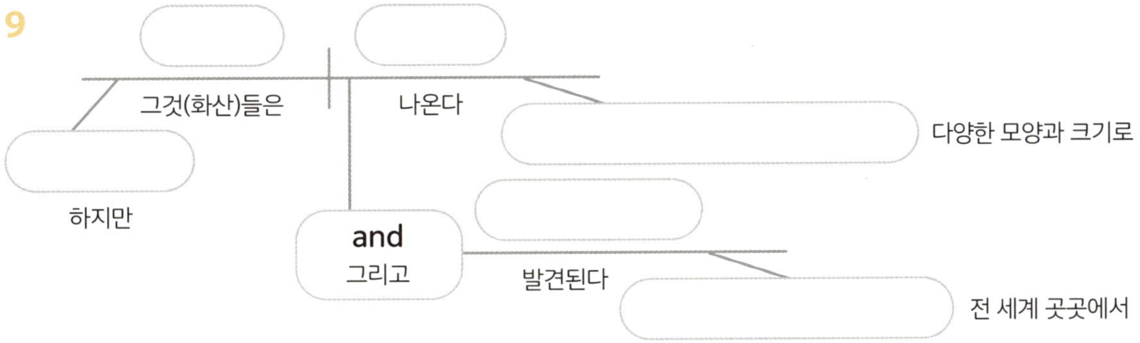

그것(화산)들은 나온다 다양한 모양과 크기로

하지만

and
그리고 발견된다 전 세계 곳곳에서

10

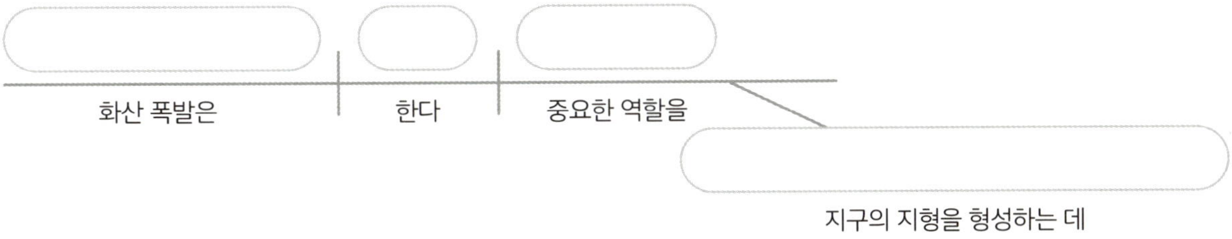

화산 폭발은 한다 중요한 역할을

지구의 지형을 형성하는 데

Step **1.** 괄호에서 문장의 흐름에 알맞은 단어나 표현 고르기
Step **2.** 해석에 맞게 끊어 읽기(/) 표시하며 문장을 읽고, 빈칸에 알맞은 해석 쓰기

TIP 읽기 속도를 높이기 위해 짧은 <(접속사 +) 주어 + 동사>는 한 덩어리로 읽기

1 The ground under your feet (seem, seems) solid,
문장의 주어는 the ground

➜ 땅은 / ______________ / ~처럼 보인다 / 단단한 //

but in some (place, places), it is weak or *cracked.
some + 셀 수 있는 명사 복수형

➜ 그러나 ______________ / 그것은 ~이다 / 약하거나 갈라져 있는

2 (These, This) weak spots (is, are) where volcanoes form.
복수 spots를 수식   주어가 복수

➜ 이런 약한 지점들이 ~이다 / ______________ 곳

3 (A, An) volcano is (an, a) opening in the Earth's crust.
an은 모음소리로 시작하는 단수명사 앞

➜ 화산은 ~이다 / 구멍 / ______________ 에 있는

4 Through this opening, (melt, melted) rock, ash, and gases (is, are) expelled.
rock을 수식하는 형용사   and로 연결된 주어는 복수 취급

➜ ______________ / 녹은 암석, 화산재, 가스가 / 분출된다

5 The *melted rock (beneath, on) the Earth's crust (is, are) called magma.
(지각) 아래에   문장의 주어는 the melted rock

______________ / 지각 아래의 / ~라고 불린다 / 마그마

6 When it (flow, flows) out of a volcano, it (is, was) called lava.
주어가 단수   과학적 사실은 현재형으로 나타냄

➜ 그것이 흐를 때 / ______________ / 그것은 ~라고 불린다 / 용암

7 Lava can sometimes (move, moves) very fast, like a red-hot river.
조동사 뒤에는 동사원형

➔ 용암은 때때로 이동할 수 있다 / 매우 빠르게 / ___________

8 Volcanoes (are often, often are) *cone-shaped mountains,
빈도부사는 be동사 뒤에

➔ 화산은 보통 ~이다 / ___________ //
formed from *(harden, hardened) lava.
명사 lava를 수식하는 형용사

➔ 굳어진 용암으로 형성된

9 However, (it comes, they come) in many shapes and (size, sizes)
앞 문장의 Volcanoes를 대신하는 주어와 동사   many의 수식을 받는 명사 복수형

➔ 하지만 / 그것(화산)들은 나온다 / ___________ //
and are (find, found) all over the world.
be동사 + 과거분사(p.p.)

➔ 그리고 발견된다 / ___________

10 Volcanic eruptions (play, plays) a key role in (shape, shaping) the Earth's landscape.
주어가 복수   전치사 in + 동명사

➔ 화산 폭발은 ~한다 / ___________ / 지구의 지형을 형성하는 데

형용사 역할을 하는 과거분사
과거분사는 「be동사 + 과거분사(p.p.)」 형태의 수동태뿐만 아니라 보어나 명사를 수식하는 형용사 역할을 할 수 있어요.

- It is weak or **cracked**.
  (보어: 갈라져 있는)

- The **melted** rock beneath the Earth's crust is called magma.
  (명사 수식: 녹은 바위)

- Volcanoes are often **cone-shaped** mountains, formed from **hardened** lava.
  (명사 수식: 원뿔 모양의 산)   (명사 수식: 굳은 용암)

Unit 20

Water

🎧 Unit 20_mp3

A 🔵 **Speed Reading** 빠르게 읽으며 내용상 중요 단어나 구라고 생각되는 부분에 동그라미 하세요.

Water is all around us. Most of it is found in seas and oceans, which cover about two-thirds of Earth's surface. Water also exists in the ground and the air. In cold places, it is frozen as ice and snow. Underground, it is stored in the soil and rocks. In the air, it becomes an invisible gas.

All water is recycled. It moves through the Earth's atmosphere, surface, and underground. When the sun warms the oceans, water turns into vapor, rising into the air to form clouds. Wind carries the clouds over the land, where the water falls as rain or snow. Rainwater flows into streams and rivers, finally returning to the oceans. Then, the cycle begins all over again.

W ords

surface 표면 ㅣ exist 존재하다 ㅣ frozen 얼어붙은 ㅣ invisible 보이지 않는 ㅣ recycle 재순환[재활용]하다 ㅣ atmosphere 대기
underground 지하 ㅣ warm 따뜻하게 하다 ㅣ vapor 증기 ㅣ rainwater 빗물 ㅣ stream 개울 ㅣ cycle 순환

B **R**eading for Information 글을 빠르게 다시 읽고, 아래 질문에 답하세요.

1 글의 내용과 일치하면 Yes, 틀리면 No에 동그라미 하세요.

1) Most of Earth's water is found in seas and oceans. **Yes** **No**

2) Water does not exist in the ground. **Yes** **No**

3) Rainwater never returns to the oceans. **Yes** **No**

2 글의 내용과 일치하도록 빈칸에 알맞은 단어를 써 보세요. (서술형)

All water is 1) r__________ through the sky, land, and 2) u__________.

3 구름 속 수증기가 어떤 형태로 땅에 떨어지는지 영어로 두 가지를 써 보세요. (서술형)

→ ____

C **C**hecking Vocabulary 단어를 영어로 바르게 설명한 것을 찾아 연결하세요.

1 surface ●   ● ⓐ tiny drops of water in the air, like steam from boiling water

2 store ●   ● ⓑ not able to be seen

3 invisible ●   ● ⓒ the top layer of something, like the ground or the water

4 recycle ●   ● ⓓ to gather and keep for future use

5 vapor ●   ● ⓔ to use something again in a new way

Step **1.** 글의 내용을 생각하며 자세하게 다시 읽기
Step **2.** 빈칸을 채우며 문장 구조 생각하기

1 Water is all around us. **2** Most of it is found in seas and oceans, which cover about two-thirds of Earth's surface. **3** Water also exists in the ground and the air. **4** In cold places, it is frozen as ice and snow. **5** Underground, it is stored in the soil and rocks. **6** In the air, it becomes an invisible gas.

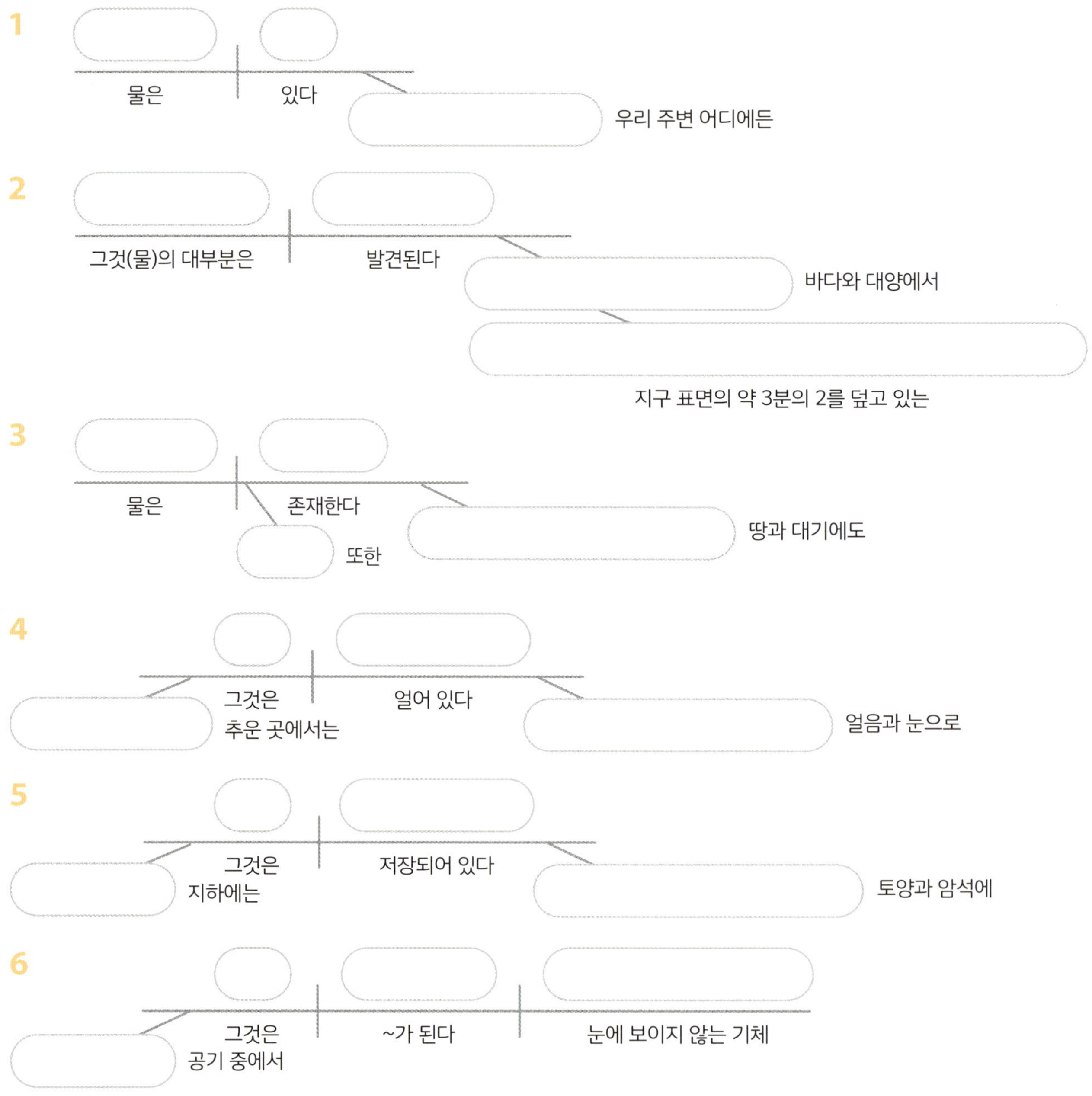

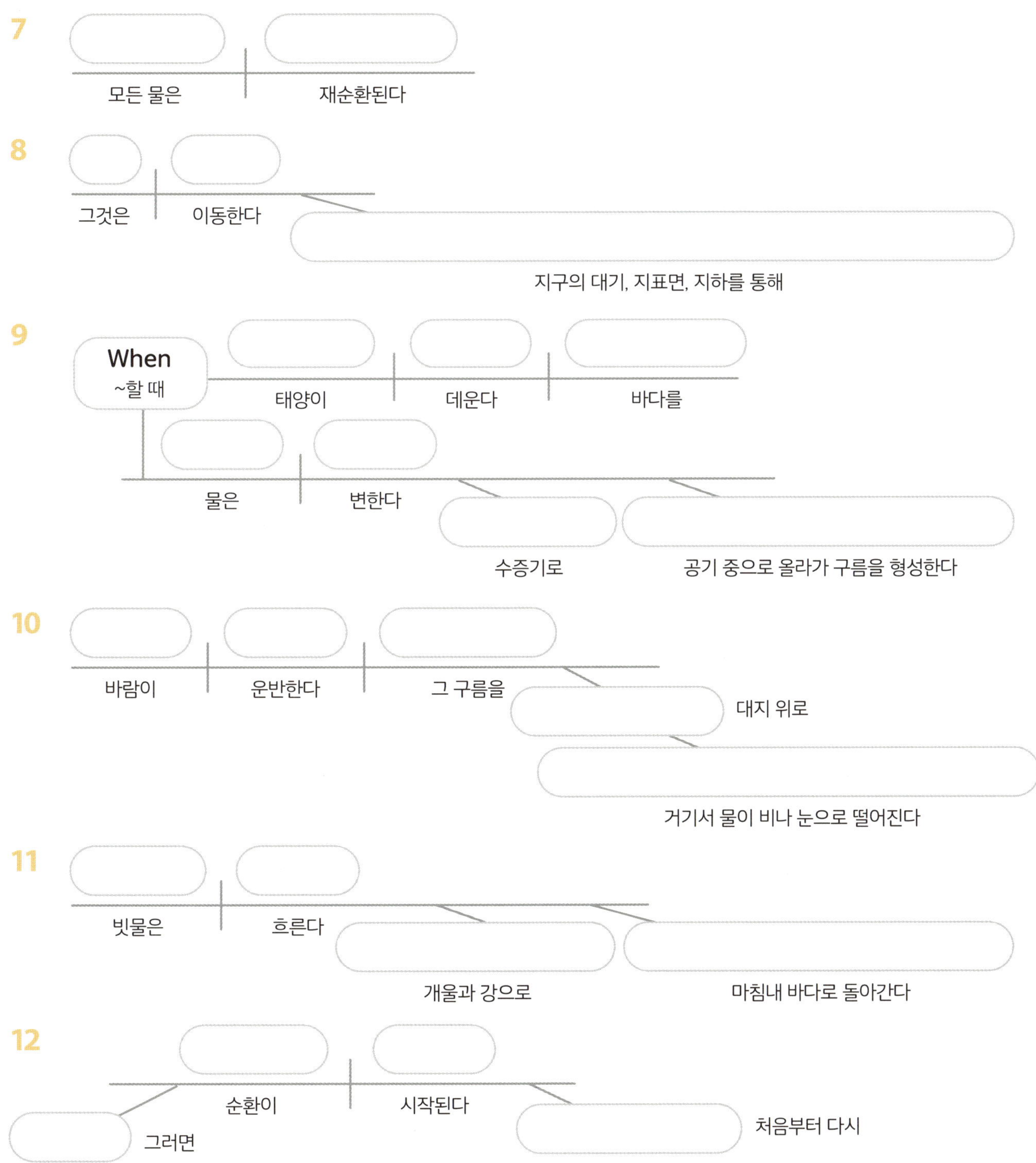
7
모든 물은
재순환된다

8
그것은
이동한다
지구의 대기, 지표면, 지하를 통해

9
When
~할 때
태양이
데운다
바다를
물은
변한다
수증기로
공기 중으로 올라가 구름을 형성한다

10
바람이
운반한다
그 구름을
대지 위로
거기서 물이 비나 눈으로 떨어진다

11
빗물은
흐른다
개울과 강으로
마침내 바다로 돌아간다

12
순환이
시작된다
그러면
처음부터 다시

Step **1.** 괄호에서 문장의 흐름에 알맞은 단어나 표현 고르기
Step **2.** 해석에 맞게 끊어 읽기(/) 표시하며 문장을 읽고, 빈칸에 알맞은 해석 쓰기

TIP 읽기 속도를 높이기 위해 짧은 <(접속사 +) 주어 + 동사>는 한 덩어리로 읽기

1　Water (is, are) all around (we, us).
주어가 단수　　전치사 뒤에는 인칭대명사 목적격

→ 물은 (~에) 있다[존재한다] / _______________

2　(Many, Most) of it *(is found, are found) in seas and oceans,
many는 형용사　　주어가 단수

→ (그것의) 대부분은 / _______________ / 바다와 대양에서 //

which (cover, covers) about (two-third, two-thirds) of Earth's surface.
주어 which는 seas와 oceans　　two는 복수형 분모(서수)와 함께

→ 덮고 있는 / 지구 표면의 _______________

3　Water also (exist, exists) in the ground and the air.
주어 water은 단수 주어

→ 물은 또한 존재한다 / _______________

4　In cold places, (it, they) *is frozen as (an ice, ice) and (snow, snows).
water을 대신하는 인칭대명사　　ice, snow는 셀 수 없는 명사

→ 추운 곳에서는 / 그것(물)이 _______________ / 얼음과 눈으로

5　Underground, it *(is stored, is store) in the soil and (rock, rocks).
수동태: be동사 + 과거분사(p.p.)　　rock은 셀 수 있는 명사

→ 지하에는 / 그것은 _______________ / 토양과 암석에

6　In the air, it (become, becomes) (a, an) invisible gas.
주어가 단수　　모음 소리 앞 관사

→ _______________ / 그것은 ~가 된다 / 눈에 보이지 않는 기체

7　All (water, waters) *is recycled.
water은 셀 수 없는 명사

→ 모든 물은 / _______________

8 It (moves, move) through the Earth's atmosphere, surface, and underground.
주어가 단수

→ 그것은 이동한다 / 지구의 대기, 지표면, 그리고 ________

9 When (a sun, the sun) warms the oceans,
sun은 세상에 하나밖에 없는 것

→ 태양이 데울 때 / ________ //

water (turn, turns) into vapor, (rise, rising) into the air to (form, forming) clouds.
주어가 단수　　　　　　　분사구문　　　　　　　to 부정사: to + 동사원형

→ 물은 변한다 / ________ / 공기 중으로 올라가 / 구름을 형성한다

10 (A wind, Wind) carries the clouds (under, over) the land,
wind는 셀 수 없는 명사　　　　　　　~ 위로

→ ________ / 그 구름을 / 대지 위로 //

where the water (fall, falls) as rain or snow.
단수 주어

→ 거기서 / 물이 떨어진다 / ________

11 Rainwater (flow, flows) into streams and rivers, finally (returns, returning) to the oceans.
주어 Rainwater는단수　　　　　　　분사구문

→ ________ / 개울과 강으로 / 마침내 돌아가다 / 바다로

12 Then, the cycle (begin, begins) all over again.
주어가 단수

→ 그러면 / ________ / 처음부터 다시

수동태의 be동사와 주어

수동태의 be동사를 쓸 때는 앞에 주어의 수(단수, 복수)에 따라 결정해요.

- **It is frozen** as ice and snow. (얼어 있다: It은 단수 주어)
- **It is stored** in the soil and rocks. (저장된다: It은 단수 주어)
- **All** water **is recycled**. (재활용된다: All water는 단수 주어)

주어에 most of 표현이 있을 때 of 뒤 명사의 수에 따라 주어 most의 수가 결정돼요.

- **Most of it is found** in seas and oceans. (발견된다: Most of it은 단수 주어)

정답 및 해석

Unit 01 · Air 공기

pp.12~17

A ·

공기는 어디에나 있다. 우리는 공기를 볼 수도, 냄새를 맡을 수도, 맛볼 수도 없지만 산들바람처럼 공기가 움직이는 것을 느낄 수는 있다. 우리는 비눗방울을 불거나 촛불을 끄기 위해 공기를 불어 넣는다. 우리는 또 풍선이나 자전거 타이어가 공기로 채워지면서 더 커지는 것도 볼 수 있다.

공기는 지구를 한 층으로 덮고 있는 기체 혼합물이다. 낮에는 공기가 태양의 해로운 광선으로부터 우리를 보호한다. 밤에는 지구를 따뜻하게 유지하는 담요와 같은 역할을 한다. 모든 사람은 숨을 쉬기 위해 공기가 필요하다. 공기는 모든 생명체가 필요로 하는 산소를 우리에게 공급한다.

B · Reading for Information

p.13

1. 1) No 2) Yes 3) No
2. 1) sun 2) day 3) Earth 4) night
3. 숨을 쉬기 위해 / 산소를 공급해 주므로

C · Checking Vocabulary

p.13

1. ⓑ 공기처럼 형태가 없고, 보통 볼 수 없는 것
2. ⓒ 나쁜, 위험한
3. ⓐ 폐 안팎으로 공기를 이동시키다
4. ⓔ 위험이나 위해로부터 방어하거나 안전하게 지키다
5. ⓓ 가는 빛의 줄기

D · Reading for Learning

pp.14~15

1. Air / is / everywhere
2. We / cannot see, smell, or taste / air
   we / can feel / it / moving / as a breeze
3. We / blow / bubbles
   blow / air / to put out a candle
4. We / can also see / a balloon or bicycle tire /
   grow bigger
   it / fills / with air
5. Air / is / a mixture of gases / that covers the Earth /
   in a layer

6. By day / air / protects / us / from the sun's harmful
   rays
7. At night / it / acts / like a blanket / to keep the Earth
   warm
8. Everyone / needs / air / to breathe
9. It / gives / us / the oxygen / that all living things need

E · Grammar for Reading

pp.16~17

1. Air **is** / everywhere. 어디에나
2. We cannot **see**, / smell, or taste / **air** 맛볼 수도 없다
   but we can feel / **it** / moving / as a breeze.
   산들바람처럼
3. We blow / **bubbles** / or **blow** / air / to **put out** a
   candle. 촛불을 끄기 위해
4. We can also see / a **balloon** or bicycle tire /
   grow **bigger** 더 커지는 것을
   as it **fills** / with air. 공기로
5. Air **is** / a mixture of gases / that **covers** the Earth /
   in a layer. 지구를 덮고 있는
6. **By** day, / air protects / **us** / from the sun's harmful
   rays. 낮에는 / 우리를
7. **At** night, / it acts / like a blanket / to **keep** the Earth
   warm. 담요와 같은
8. Everyone **needs** / air / to **breathe**. 숨을 쉬기 위해
9. It gives / **us** / the oxygen / that all living things
   need. 우리에게 / 산소를

Unit 02 · Bats 박쥐

pp.18~23

A ·

박쥐는 날개가 달린 작고 털이 있는 포유류이다. 박쥐는 날 수 있는 유일한 포유류이다. 대부분의 박쥐는 밤에만 날아다닌다. 낮 동안에는 동굴, 다락, 헛간 또는 나무에 거꾸로 매달려 쉰다. 박쥐는 900종 이상이 있으며 일부는 멸종 위기에 처해 있다.

대부분의 박쥐는 군집이라고 불리는 무리를 지어 산다. 박쥐는 찍찍거리는 소리를 내서 주변에서 길을 찾는다. 이 소리는 박쥐의 민감한 귀가 들을 수 있는 메아리로 되돌아온다. 추운 기후에서 박쥐

는 더 따뜻한 지역으로 이동하거나 동면한다. 동면 중 박쥐의 몸은
에너지를 많이 사용하지 않기 때문에 음식을 거의 먹지 않는다.

B   p.19

1. 1) Yes 2) No 3) Yes
2. 1) colonies 2) move 3) hibernate
3. 박쥐는 날 수 있는 유일한 포유류이다.

C   p.19

1. ⓒ 털이 있는 외피를 가지고 있는
2. ⓓ 가까이에서 함께 사는 같은 종류의 동물들
3. ⓔ 피부에 털이나 모발이 있고, 새끼에게 젖을 먹이는 온혈
    동물
4. ⓑ 에너지를 절약하기 위해 겨울 동안 잠을 자다
5. ⓐ 사라질 위험에 처한

D   pp.20~21

1. Bats / are / small, furry mammals / with wings
2. They / are / the only mammals / that can fly
3. Most bats / fly / only at night
4. They / rest / during the day / hanging upside down /
    in caves, attics, barns, or trees
5. are / more than 900 kinds of bats
    some / are / endangered
6. Most bats / live / in groups / called colonies
7. They / find / their way / around / by making squeaks
8. These sounds / bounce back / as echoes / that their
    sensitive ears can hear
9. In cold climates / bats / either move / to warmer
    areas
    or hibernate
10. During hibernation / their bodies / do not use /
    much energy
    they / eat / little food

E   pp.22~23

1. Bats **are** / small, furry mammals / **with** wings. 작고
    털이 있는 포유류
2. **They** are / the only mammals / that can **fly**. 날 수 있는

3. Most **bats** fly / only **at** night. 대부분의 박쥐는
4. They rest / **during** the day, / **hanging** upside down
    / **in** caves, attics, barns, or trees. 낮 동안 / 나무에
5. There are / **more** than 900 kinds of bats, /
    and some **are** / endangered. 박쥐가
6. Most bats **live** / in groups / **called** colonies.
    무리를 지어
7. They find / **their** way / around / by **making** squeaks.
    그것들은 찾는다
8. **These** sounds / bounce back / as echoes / that their
    sensitive ears can **hear**. 메아리로
9. In cold climates, / bats either move / **to** warmer
    areas / **or** hibernate.
    추운 기후에서 / 더 따뜻한 지역으로
10. **During** hibernation, / their bodies / **do** not use /
    much energy, 사용하지 않는다
    so they eat / **little** food. 그래서

A

우리 몸은 다양한 종류의 세포로 이루어진 공장처럼 작동한다. 세
포는 모양과 크기가 다양하고, 할 일도 다르다. 세포는 피부, 심장,
혈액, 근육, 뼈와 같은 우리의 신체 부위를 형성한다. 이 모든 부분
은 "공장"이 원활하게 돌아가도록 함께 작동한다.
인체는 성장하고 스스로 치유하기 위해 새로운 세포를 생성한다.
세포는 스스로를 복제한다. 우리 몸은 매일 수백만 개의 세포를 교
체한다. 일생 우리 몸은 수많은 머리카락과 혈액, 피부를 생성한다.
우리의 몸은 성장하고 기능하기 위해 음식과 물, 산소가 필요하다.

B   p.25

1. 1) No 2) Yes 3) No
2. cells
3. 음식, 물, 산소

C   p.25

1. ⓑ 제품이 만들어지는 큰 건물

2. ⓐ 뼈가 움직이게 하는 동물과 인간의 부드러운 살 조각들

3. ⓔ 건강하거나 온전한 상태가 되게 하다

4. ⓒ 다른 것과 똑같아 보이는 것

5. ⓓ 한 사람이 살아있는 동안

D Reading for Learning   pp.26~27

1. Our body / works / like a factory / with many types of cells

2. The cells / come / in different shapes and sizes have / different jobs / to do

3. They / form / the parts of our body / such as the skin heart, blood, muscles, and bones

4. All these parts / work / together / to keep the "factory" running smoothly

5. The human body / creates / new cells / to grow and heal itself

6. Cells / make / copies of themselves

7. Our body / replaces / millions of cells / every day

8. Over a lifetime / it / produces / a lot of hair, blood, and skin

9. Our body / needs / food, water, and oxygen / to grow and function

---

E Grammar for Reading   pp.28~29

1. Our body **works** / like a factory / with **many** types of cells. 공장처럼

2. The cells come / in **different** shapes and sizes 다양한 모양과 크기로
and / **have** / different jobs / to do. 다양한 역할들을

3. They **form** / the parts of our body / such as the skin heart, **blood**, muscles, and bones. 우리 몸의 부위를

4. All these **parts** / work together / to keep the "factory" running **smoothly**. 함께 작동한다

5. The human body **creates** / new cells / **to grow** and heal itself. 새로운 세포를 / 치료하기 위해

6. Cells **make** / copies of **themselves**. 자신의 복사본을

7. Our body replaces / **millions** of cells / **every day**. 수백만 개의 세포를 / 매일

8. Over a lifetime / **it** produces / **a lot of** hair, blood, and skin. 일생

---

9. Our body **needs** / food, water, and oxygen **/ to grow** and function. 음식, 물, 산소를

Unit 04 **Clothes** 옷   pp.30~35

A Speed Reading

옷은 유용하다. 인간은 몸을 보호하기 위해 옷이 필요하다. 사람들은 몸을 따뜻하게 유지하고, 시원하게 지내고, 스포츠를 하거나 학교에 가기 위해 다양한 옷을 입는다. 옷은 당신을 멋지게 보이게 할 수 있다. 스타일과 패션에 관한 생각은 항상 변화하고 있다. 이는 나라마다, 그리고 인류 역사에 걸쳐 달라진다.

옷은 다양한 여러 가지 재료로 만들어진다. 수 세기 동안 모든 직물은 누에에서 얻은 비단, 식물에서 얻은 리넨과 면, 양에서 얻은 양모처럼 자연적인 것에서 나왔다. 1800년대 후반엔 사람들이 인공 섬유를 만들기 시작했다. 1980년대에는 다시 사람들이 천연 섬유를 사용하기 시작했다.

B Reading for Information   p.31

1. 1) Yes   2) No   3) No

2. 1) Artificial 2) natural

3. silk, linen, cotton, wool

C Checking Vocabulary   p.31

1. ⓑ 자연스럽지 않은, 인간에 의해 만들어진

2. ⓒ 울이나 면과 같은 어떤 것의 가느다란 실

3. ⓔ 짜거나 뜨개질한 재료, 천

4. ⓐ 특정 시기에 인기 있는 옷 입기 방식

5. ⓓ 변화하다, 다르거나 달라지다

D Reading for Learning   pp.32~33

1. Clothes / are / useful

2. Humans / need / clothes / to protect their bodies

3. People / wear / different clothes / to keep warm, stay cool, play sports, or go to school

4. Clothes / can make / you / look good

5. Ideas / about style and fashion / are always changing

6. They / vary / from one country to another /
throughout human history

7. Clothes / are made / from many different materials

8. For centuries / all fabrics / came / from natural
things / silk from silkworms, linen and cotton from
plants, and wool from sheep

9. In the late 1800s / people / started / making artificial
fibers

10. In the 1980s / people / began / to use natural fibers /
again

E **Grammar for Reading** pp.34~35

1. Clothes **are** / useful. 유용한

2. Humans **need** / clothes / to protect **their** bodies.
몸을 보호하기 위해

3. People **wear** / different clothes 사람들은 입는다
to keep warm, stay cool, play sports, or **go** to school.
학교에 가기 위해

4. Clothes can make / **you** / look **good**. 멋지게 보이게

5. Ideas about style and fashion / **are** always **changing**. 스타일과 패션에 대한 생각들은

6. They **vary** / from one country **to** another / and
throughout human history. 나라마다

7. Clothes are **made** / from many different **materials**.
옷은 만들어진다

8. **For** centuries, / all **fabrics** came / from natural
things // 수 세기 동안
silk **from** silkworms, linen and cotton from **plants**, and
wool from **sheep**. 누에에서 얻은 비단

9. **In** the late 1800s, / people started / **making** artificial
fibers. 1800년대 후반에

10. **In** the 1980s / people **began** / to use natural fibers /
again. 천연 섬유를 사용하기

A **Speed Reading**

사막은 지구상에서 가장 건조한 곳으로 비가 거의 내리지 않는다.
낮 동안 사막은 타는 듯이 더울 수 있지만, 밤에는 얼어붙을 듯이
추워질 수도 있다. 사막에는 모래 언덕, 바위 언덕 또는 평평한 평
원이 있을 수 있다.

사막은 아무것도 없어 보이지만 많은 식물과 동물이 살고 있다. 선
인장 같은 사막 식물은 두꺼운 줄기에 물을 저장한다. 낙타는 며칠
동안 음식이나 물 없이 지낼 수 있다. 낙타는 등에 있는 혹에 지방
을 저장한다. 사막에 있는 사람들은 이동하는 동안 보통 천막에서
생활한다. 그들은 물을 찾아서 종종 오아시스 근처에 머무른다.

B **Reading for Information** p.37

1. 1) No   2) No   3) Yes

2. 1) hot   2) cold   3) plants

3. 낙타, 선인장

C **Checking Vocabulary** p.37

1. ⓑ 바다 근처나 사막에 있는 모래 언덕

2. ⓒ 나중에 사용하기 위해 무언가를 따로 보관하다

3. ⓐ 건조한 지역에서 자라는 식물

4. ⓔ (낙타와 같은) 동물의 등에 있는 혹

5. ⓓ 사막에서 물과 식물이 발견되는 장소

D **Reading for Learning** pp.38~39

1. Deserts / are / the driest places / on Earth
receive / very little rain

2. During the day / deserts / can be / baking hot
at night / they / can become / freezing cold

3. Deserts / can have / sand dunes, rocky hills, or flat
plains

4. deserts / seem / empty
many plants and animals / live / there

5. Desert plants / like cacti / store / water / in their
thick stems

6. Camels / can go / for days / without food or water

7. They / store / fat / in the humps / on their backs

8. People / in deserts / usually / live / in tents / while traveling

9. They / often / stay / near oases / in search of water

E Grammar for Reading   pp.40~41

1. Deserts **are** / the driest places on Earth / and receive / very **little** rain. 가장 건조한 곳

2. **During** the day / deserts can **be** / baking hot, 낮 동안

but **at** night / **they** can become / freezing cold. 얼어붙을 듯이 추운

3. **Deserts** can **have** / sand dunes, **rocky** hills, or flat plains. 바위 언덕

4. Even though deserts **seem** / empty 텅 비어 있는 **many** plants and animals / live / there. 식물과 동물이

5. Desert plants, like cacti / **store** / **water** / in their thick stems. 저장한다 / 물을

6. Camels can **go** / for days / **without food** or water. 음식이나 물 없이

7. They **store** / fat / in the humps / **on** their backs. 지방을

8. People **in** deserts / **usually live** / in tents / while **traveling**. 천막에서

9. They **often stay** / near oases / in search of water. 오아시스 근처에

Unit
06 **Eating** 식사   pp.42~47

A Speed Reading

음식은 사람에게 에너지를 제공한다. 음식은 성장에 도움이 되고 건강을 유지하게 해준다. 사람의 몸은 배고픔을 느끼게 하여 음식이 필요하다는 것을 알려준다. 사람은 먹을 때 음식을 씹고 삼킨다. 이를 통해 사람의 몸은 음식에서 영양분을 모을 수 있다. 그런 다음 남은 음식물은 소화 기관을 통해 이동한다.

소화는 입에서 시작된다. 씹을 때 음식물은 침이라고 하는 액체와 섞인다. 침은 음식물을 묽은 덩어리로 분해하기 시작한다. 그런 다음 소화 기관 내의 특수 세포가 영양분을 흡수한다. 마지막으로 냄새나는 음식물 찌꺼기는 수십억 마리의 죽은 박테리아와 함께 몸 밖으로 배출될 준비가 된다.

B Reading for Information   p.43

1. 1) Yes   2) No   3) Yes

2. 1) mouth   2) digestion   3) nutrients

3. 배고픈 것을 느끼게 함으로써

C Checking Vocabulary   p.43

1. ⓑ 일을 하거나 변화를 일으키는 능력

2. ⓐ 음식을 치아로 잘게 부수다

3. ⓔ 음식에 있으며 사람, 동물, 식물이 살아가고 성장하는 데 도움이 되는 것

4. ⓒ 액체나 기체, 열을 받아들여 유지하다

5. ⓓ 무엇인가에서 나오거나 떠나다

D Reading for Learning   pp.44~45

1. Food / gives / you / energy

2. It / helps / you / grow
keeps / you / healthy

3. Your body / lets / you / know that it needs food / by making you feel hungry

4. you / eat
you / chew and swallow / the food

5. This / allows / your body / to collect nutrients / from the food

6. The leftovers / then / travel / through your digestive system

7. Digestion / begins / in the mouth

8. you / chew
food / mixes / with a liquid / called saliva

9. It / starts / breaking down food / into a watery mush

10. Special cells / in your digestive system / then / absorb / the nutrients

11. Finally / the smelly leftovers / along with billions of dead bacteria / are / ready / to exit the body

1. Food **gives** / you / **energy**. 에너지를

2. It helps / **you** grow / and keeps / you **healthy**.
   네가 성장하도록

3. Your body lets / you / **know** that it needs food / by
   making you feel hungry. 배고픔을 느끼게 함으로써

4. **When** you eat, / you chew and **swallow** / the food.
   씹고 삼킨다

5. This **allows** / your body / **to collect** nutrients / from
   the food. 영양분을 모으도록

6. The leftovers / then **travel** / through your digestive
   system. 소화 기관을 통해

7. Digestion begins / **in** the mouth. 입안에서

8. As you chew, / **food** mixes / with a liquid / **called**
   saliva. 액체와

9. **It** starts / breaking down food / into a **watery** mush.
   음식을 분해하기

10. Special cells / in your digestive system / then
    absorb / the nutrients. 너의 소화 기관 내의

11. **Finally**, / the smelly leftovers, / along with billions of
    dead bacteria, 냄새나는 남은 음식물은
    are / ready / **to exit** the body. 몸 밖으로 배출이 될

Unit 07 Family 가족
pp.48~53

A   Speed Reading

당신과 함께 살고 있는 사람들이 당신의 가족이다. 가족은 다양한
활동을 함께 한다. 함께 먹고, 놀고, 이야기하고, 집안일을 한다. 가
족은 온갖 형태와 규모로 존재한다. 대가족도 있지만, 한 부모에
한두 명의 자녀만 있는 소규모 가족도 있다. 심지어 반려동물도 가
족의 일원이 될 수 있다.

당신의 몸은 모든 세포에서 발견되는 유전자라 불리는 명령에 따
라 기능하고 성장한다. 이 유전자는 친부모로부터, 즉 절반은 어머
니, 절반은 아버지에게서 물려받는다. 일란성 쌍둥이는 같은 유전
자를 공유하기 때문에 완전히 똑같아 보인다.

1. 1) No   2) Yes   3) No

2. genes

3. 같은 유전자를 가지고 있기 때문에

1. ⓒ 청소, 세탁, 다림질과 같이 누군가 가정에서 반드시 해야 하는
   일들

2. ⓐ 신체적 특징, 성장, 발달을 조절하는 세포의 부분

3. ⓔ 생명체의 몸과 세포 안에서 일어나는 과정과 상태를 설명
   할 때 사용되는

4. ⓑ 완전히 동일한

5. ⓓ 누군가가 당신에게 하라고 말하는 것

1. The people / you live with / are / your family

2. Families / engage / in various activities together

3. They / eat, play, talk, and do chores / together

4. Families / come / in all shapes and sizes

5. Some / are / large
   others / are / small / with just one parent and one or
   two children

6. Even / pets / can be / part of a family

7. Your body / functions and grows / based on
   instructions called genes / which are found in all
   your cells

8. These genes / are inherited / from your biological
   parents / half coming from your mother / half from
   your father

9. Identical twins / look / exactly alike
   they / share / the same genes

1. The people / you live with / **are** / your family.
   네가 함께 사는

2. Families **engage** / in various activities / together.
   다양한 활동에

3. They **eat**, / play, talk, and **do** chores / together.
   집안일을

4. Families **come** / in all **shapes** and sizes. 형태와 규모로

5. Some **are** / large,
while **others** are / small, / with just one **parent** and
one or two **children**. 한 부모와

6. Even pets / can **be** / part of a family. 가족의 일원이

7. Your body / **functions** and **grows** / based on
instructions / called genes, 명령에 따라
which are found / in all your **cells**. 모든 세포

8. These genes **are** inherited / **from** your biological
parents 친부모로부터
half coming **from** your mother / **and** half from your
father. 절반은 아버지에게서

9. Identical twins **look** / exactly alike 완전히 똑같은
because **they** share / the **same** genes. 같은 유전자를

Unit 08 Feelings 감정

pp.54~59

A Speed Reading

우리는 여러 감정들을 가질 수 있다. 우리는 행복하거나 슬프고,
흥분하거나 지루함을 느낄 수도 있다. 가끔 평온하거나 화가 날 수
도 있다. 우리는 다양한 방식으로 감정을 표현한다. 예를 들어 우리
가 웃을 때, 그것은 다른 사람들에게 우리가 재미있어하고 있다는
것을 보여주는 것이다. 때로 우리는 매우 행복할 때조차 운다.

누구나 감정은 있지만, 사람들이 같은 방식으로 느끼는 것은 아니
다. 어떤 사람들은 혼자 시간 보내는 것을 좋아하지만, 다른 사람
들은 잠깐만 혼자 있어도 외로움을 느낀다. 어떤 사람들은 거미를
좋아하지만, 다른 사람들은 거미를 무서워한다. 어떤 사람들은 무
서운 영화를 보거나 롤러코스터 타는 것을 즐기는데, 그들은 무서
운 기분의 전율을 좋아하기 때문이다!

B Reading for Information

p.55

1. 1) No   2) Yes   3) No

2. feelings

3. 무서운 기분의 전율을 좋아해서

C Checking Vocabulary

p.55

1. ⓐ 흥분하거나 화나지 않은

2. ⓐ 분노나 행복과 같은 감정

3. ⓑ 두려움을 일으키는, 무서운

4. ⓒ 흥분이나 기쁨의 강한 감정

5. ⓔ 꼬불꼬불한 트랙을 개방된 열차가 오르내리는 놀이공원
기구

D Reading for Learning

pp.56~57

1. We / can have / many feelings

2. We / might feel / happy or sad, excited or bored

3. Sometimes / we / can feel / calm or angry

4. We / show / our feelings / in different ways

5. For example / we laugh /
it / shows / others / that we are having fun

6. Sometimes / we / cry
we / feel / very happy

7. Everyone / has / feelings
people / don't feel / the same way

8. Some people / love / spending time alone
others / feel / lonely / even after a short time alone

9. Some people / like / spiders
others / are / afraid / of them

10. Some people / enjoy / watching scary movies or
taking roller coaster rides
they / like / the thrill / of feeling scared

E Grammar for Reading

pp.58~59

1. We can have / **many** feelings. 많은 감정을

2. We might feel / happy or **sad**, excited or **bored**.
우리는 느낄지도 모른다

3. Sometimes / we can feel / **calm** or angry.
우리는 느낄 수 있다

4. We show / **our** feelings / in different ways.
우리의 감정을

5. For example, / when we laugh, 예를 들어
it **shows** / others / that we are **having** fun.
우리가 재미있어하고 있다는 것을

6. Sometimes / we cry / even when we feel / very
happy. 우리는 운다

7. Everyone **has** / feelings, / but people **don't** feel /
the same way. 같은 방식으로

8. Some **people** love **/ spending** time alone,
혼자 시간 보내는 것을
while **others** feel **/** lonely **/** even after a short time
alone.

9. Some people **like /** spiders, 어떤 사람들은 좋아한다
while others are **/** afraid of **them**.

10. Some people enjoy **/ watching** scary movies or
taking roller coaster rides 롤러코스터 타는 것을
because they like **/** the thrill of **feeling** scared!

Unit 09 Flowers 꽃

pp.60~65

A Speed Reading

꽃은 열매나 씨앗을 생산하는 식물의 일부이다. 꽃은 흔히 밝은색과 기분 좋은 냄새를 갖고 있다. 씨앗을 만들려면 수술에서 나온 꽃가루가 암술머리에 내려앉아야 한다. 이 과정을 수분이라고 한다. 수분은 두 개의 다른 꽃 사이에서 또는 같은 꽃 안에서 일어날 수 있다.

꽃은 다양한 방식으로 수분이 된다. 일부 아주 작은 꽃가루 알갱이들은 바람에 의해 운반된다. 다른 것들은 색깔과 향기로 곤충을 유인한다. 꽃은 또한 꽃꿀이라는 달콤한 액체를 생산한다. 곤충이 꽃꿀을 마시는 동안 꽃가루가 곤충의 몸에 달라붙어 꽃에서 꽃으로 옮기게 된다.

B Reading for Information
p.61

1. 1) No   2) Yes   3) Yes
2. Pollination
3. 바람, 곤충

C Checking Vocabulary
p.61

1. ⓒ 꽃이 만드는 고운 노란색의 가루
2. ⓔ 꽃가루를 만드는 꽃의 부분
3. ⓐ 꽃가루를 받는 꽃의 부분
4. ⓑ 식물이 만드는 달콤한 액체
5. ⓓ 사람이나 동물이 가까이 오고 싶어 하게 만들다

D Reading for Learning
pp.62~63

1. A flower / is / the part of a plant / that produces fruit or seeds
2. Flowers / often / have / bright colors and a pleasant smell
3. To make a seed / pollen / from a stamen / must land / on a stigma
4. This process / is called / pollination
5. It / can occur / between two different flowers / within the same flower
6. Flowers / are pollinated / in various ways
7. Some tiny pollen grains / are carried / by the wind
8. Others / attract / insects / with their color and scent
9. Flowers / also / produce / a sugary liquid / called nectar
10. insects / drink / the nectar
pollen / sticks / to their bodies
allowing / them / to carry it / from flower to flower

E Grammar for Reading
pp.64~65

1. A flower **is /** the part **of** a plant **/** that produces fruit or **seeds**. 식물의 일부
2. Flowers **often have /** bright colors and a pleasant **smell**. 밝은 색상과
3. To make a seed, **/** pollen **from** a stamen **/** must **land /** on a stigma. 씨앗을 만들기 위해서
4. This process **/** is **called /** pollination. 수분
5. It can **occur /** between two different **flowers /** or within the same flower. 같은 꽃 내에서
6. Flowers **are** pollinated **/ in** various ways.
다양한 방식으로
7. Some tiny pollen **grains /** are carried **/ by** the wind.
바람에 의해
8. Others **attract /** insects **/ with their** color and scent.
다른 꽃들은 유인한다
9. Flowers also **produce /** a **sugary** liquid **/** called nectar. 꽃은 또한 생산한다
10. While insects **drink /** the nectar,
pollen **sticks /** to **their** bodies, 꽃가루가 달라붙는다

allowing / them / to carry it / **from** flower **to** flower.
꽃에서 꽃으로

Unit 10 Forest 숲

pp.66~71

A Speed Reading

숲은 많은 나무와 식물이 있는 넓은 면적의 땅이다. 숲은 지구 육지의 30% 이상을 덮고 있다. 숲에는 활엽수와 침엽수라는 두 가지 주요 유형의 나무가 있다. 활엽수는 잎이 넓지만, 침엽수는 바늘 모양의 잎을 가지고 있으며 원뿔 모양의 열매에 씨앗을 맺는다.

숲은 생명체에게 필수적이다. 숲은 새와 다른 동물들에게 먹이와 보금자리를 제공한다. 숲의 나무는 산소 공급을 증가시킨다. 숲의 토양은 거대한 스펀지처럼 작용한다. 숲의 토양이 비를 흡수하면 비는 땅속으로 천천히 스며들게 된다. 숲은 또한 연료와 주택 건설, 종이 제조를 위한 목재를 제공한다.

B Reading for Information

p.67

1. 1) No   2) No   3) Yes
2. 1) forest   2) shelter   3) oxygen
3. 활엽수와 침엽수

C Checking Vocabulary

p.67

1. © 열이나 동력을 제공하기 위해 태우는 나무나 휘발유 같은 것
2. ⓔ 서서히 퍼지거나 흘러 들어가다
3. ⓐ 사람이나 동물을 나쁜 날씨나 위험으로부터 보호하기 위해 만들어진 장소
4. ⓑ 누군가가 가지고 있거나 사용할 수 있는 것의 양
5. ⓓ 집을 짓거나 가구를 만드는 데 사용되는 나무

D Reading for Learning

pp.68~69

1. A forest / is / a large area of land / with many trees and plants
2. Forests / cover / more / than 30 percent of the Earth's land
3. are / two main types of trees / in forests /

hardwoods and softwoods

4. Hardwoods / have / broad leaves
   softwoods / have / needle-shaped leaves
   bear / seeds / in cones
5. Forests / are / essential / for living things
6. They / provide / food and shelter / for birds and other animals
7. Forest trees / increase / the supply of oxygen
8. Forest soils / act / like giant sponges
9. They / soak up / rain
   it / seeps / slowly / into the ground
10. Forests / also / provide / timber / for fuel, building houses, and making paper

E Grammar for Reading

pp.70~71

1. **A forest** is / a large area of land / with many **trees** and plants. 많은 나무와 식물
2. Forests **cover** / more **than** / 30 percent of the Earth's land. 지구 육지의
3. There **are** / two main types of trees / **in** forests: / hardwoods **and** softwoods. 활엽수와 침엽수
4. Hardwoods **have** / broad **leaves**, 넓은 잎을 **while** softwoods have / needle-shaped leaves / and **bear** / seeds / in cones. 바늘 모양의 잎을
5. Forests **are** / essential / **for** living things. 필수적인
6. They provide / **food** and shelter / for **birds** and other animals. 먹이와 보금자리
7. Forest trees **increase** / the supply **of** oxygen. 산소의 공급을
8. Forest soils **act** / like giant **sponges**. 거대한 스펀지처럼
9. They soak up / rain, / **so** it seeps / **slowly** / into the ground. 땅속으로
10. Forests also provide / timber / **for** fuel, **building** houses, and making paper. 목재를

Unit 11 · Friends 친구
pp.72~77

A Speed Reading

친구란 우리가 알고, 좋아하고, 신뢰하는 사람이다. 좋은 친구를 사귀고, 친구가 된다는 것은 특별한 느낌이다. 친구끼리는 보통 공통점이 많다. 이것은 우리가 서로를 이해하고 함께 즐겁게 지내는 데 도움이 된다. 친구는 함께 무언가를 하고 서로 돕는 것을 즐긴다.

그러나, 친구끼리는 서로 아주 다를 수도 있다. 연장자들이 나이가 더 어린 사람들과 친구가 될 수도 있다. 누군가와 몇 번 이야기를 하거나 놀다 보면 친구를 찾을 수도 있다. 다툴 수도 있지만 배려를 멈추지 않는다. 진정한 친구는 우리를 이해하고 성장할 수 있게 도와준다. 친구는 우리가 선택하는 가족이다.

B Reading for Information
p.73

1. 1) No   2) Yes   3) No
2. 1) common   2) understand   3) fun
3. 몇 차례 대화를 하거나 (함께) 놀기

C Checking Vocabulary
p.73

1. ⓑ ~의 의미를 이해하다, ~의 방식과 본질을 잘 알고 있다
2. ⓒ 다른 사람과 공유된
3. ⓐ 누군가에게 애정을 갖다
4. ⓔ 의견 차이를 표현하다, 다투다
5. ⓓ 나이가 많거나 나이 들어가는

D Reading for Learning
pp.74~75

1. A friend / is / someone / we know, like, and trust
2. It / is / a special feeling
   to have a good friend
   to be one
3. Friends / usually / have / a lot / in common
4. This / helps / us / understand each other
   have fun together
5. Friends / enjoy / doing things together
   helping each other
6. However / friends / can be / quite / different / from
   one another

7. Elderly people / can be / friends / with younger
   people
8. You / may find / a friend / after talking to or playing
   with someone / a few times
9. You / may argue
   you / do not stop / caring
10. True friends / understand / us
    help / us / grow
11. Friends / are / the family / we choose

E Grammar for Reading
pp.76~77

1. A **friend** is / someone / we know, like, and **trust**.
   우리가 알고
2. **It** is / a special feeling / to have a good friend / and
   to be one. 친구가 된다는 것은
3. Friends **usually have** / a lot / in common. 공통적으로
4. This helps / **us** / understand each other / and **have**
   fun together. 서로 이해하도록
5. Friends **enjoy** / doing things together / and **helping**
   each other. 친구들은 즐긴다
6. However, / friends can **be** / quite different / **from**
   one another. 아주 다른
7. Elderly people / can be / friends / **with** younger
   people. 더 젊은 사람들과
8. You may **find** / a friend / after **talking** to or playing
   with someone / a few times. 너는 찾을 수도 있다
9. You may argue, / but you **do** not stop / **caring**.
   너는 멈추지 않는다
10. True friends **understand** / us / and help / us / **grow**.
    진정한 친구들은 이해한다
11. Friends **are** / the family / we choose. 우리가 선택하는

Unit 12 · Kangaroos 캥거루
pp.78~83

A Speed Reading

캥거루는 뒷다리로 뛰어 이동하는 호주의 대형 동물이다. 캥거루는 큰 귀, 강한 뒷다리, 짧은 앞다리, 긴 꼬리를 가진 초식 동물이

다. 캥거루는 시속 30마일까지 달릴 수 있다. 캥거루는 달릴 때 균형을 잡기 위해 두꺼운 꼬리를 들어 올린다.

암컷 캥거루는 몸 앞쪽에 큰 주머니를 가지고 있는데, 여기서 새끼가 자란다. 캥거루 새끼는 주머니 안에서 약 6개월을 보낸다. 새끼는 한 살이 될 때까지 어미의 젖을 계속 먹는다. 수컷 캥거루들은 누가 우두머리인지 결정하기 위해 서로 싸운다. 승자가 그 무리의 지도자가 된다.

B Reading for Information   p.79

1. 1) No   2) Yes   3) No

2. 1) pouch   2) milk

3. 몸의 균형을 잡는 것을 도와준다.

C Checking Vocabulary   p.79

1. ⓑ 그룹을 이끌고 결정하는 존재

2. ⓒ 넘어지지 않도록 몸을 안정적으로 유지하는 법

3. ⓓ 새끼를 낳을 수 있는 성별의 사람이나 동물, 여성 또는 여자아이

4. ⓔ 일부 암컷 동물에게 있는 새끼를 담고 운반하는 데 사용되는 자연적인 피부 주머니

5. ⓐ 계속 일어나다, 지속하다

D Reading for Learning   pp.80~81

1. A kangaroo / is / a large Australian animal / that moves / by jumping on its back legs

2. It / is / a plant-eating animal / with large ears, strong back legs, short front legs, and a long tail

3. A kangaroo / can run / up to 30 miles an hour

4. it / runs
it / holds up / its thick tail / for balance

5. A female kangaroo / has / a big pouch / in the front of her body / where her baby grows

6. The baby / spends / about six months / inside the pouch

7. It / continues / to drink its mother's milk
it / is / a year old

8. Male kangaroos / fight / each other / to decide who is boss

9. The winner / becomes / the leader / of the group

E Grammar for Reading   pp.82~83

1. A kangaroo **is** / a large Australian animal
호주의 대형 동물
that **moves** / by **jumping** on its back legs. 뒷다리로

2. It is / **a** plant-eating animal / **with** large ears, strong back **legs**, short front legs, **and** a long **tail**. 큰 귀, 강한 뒷다리, 짧은 앞다리

3. A kangaroo **can run** / up to 30 miles **an** hour.
캥거루는 달릴 수 있다

4. **As** it runs, / it **holds** up / its thick tail / **for** balance.
두꺼운 꼬리를

5. A **female** kangaroo has / a big pouch / **in** the front of **her** body, 큰 주머니를
where her baby **grows**. 새끼가 자란다

6. The baby **spends** / about six **months** / inside the pouch. 약 6개월을

7. It continues / **to drink** its mother's milk / until it is a **year** old. 한 살이 될 때까지

8. Male kangaroos **fight** / each other / **to decide** who **is** boss. 누가 우두머리인지

9. The winner **becomes** / the leader / **of** the group.
승자는 ~된다

Unit 13 Learning 배움   pp.84~89

A Speed Reading

배움이란 어떤 것들에 대해 알아가는 과정이다. 배움은 주변 세상을 이해하는 데 도움이 된다. 이는 개인의 성장과 발전으로 이어진다. 우리는 새로운 지식과 기술, 태도, 행동을 배울 수 있다. 배우는 방법에는 여러 가지가 있다. 우리는 경험과 공부, 가르침을 통해, 심지어 실수를 통해 배울 수 있다.

배움은 항상 일어난다. 어떤 일은 매우 빨리 배울 수 있다. 읽기나 쓰기와 같이 더 어려운 기술은 훨씬 더 오랜 시간이 걸릴 수 있고 도움이 필요할 수도 있다. 배움은 평생의 여정이다. 우리는 평생에 걸쳐 모든 종류의 것들을 계속 배우게 될 것이다. 더 많이 배울수록 인생은 더 흥미로워진다.

B   Reading for Information   p.85

1. 1) No   2) Yes   3) No

2. learn

3. 기술, 태도, 행동

C   Checking Vocabulary   p.85

1. ⓒ 어떤 일을 하거나 목표에 도달하기 위한 일련의 행동

2. ⓓ 어떤 것 또는 누군가에 대해 느끼거나 생각하는 방식

3. ⓔ 옳지 않은 생각이나 행동, 오류

4. ⓐ 사람의 인생 전체에 걸쳐 계속되는

5. ⓑ 한 장소에서 다른 장소로의 긴 여행

D   Reading for Learning   pp.86~87

1. Learning / is / the process / of finding out about things

2. It / helps / you / understand the world around you

3. It / leads / to personal growth and development

4. You / can learn / new knowledge, skills, attitudes, or behaviors

5. are / different ways / to learn

6. You / can learn / by experience, study, or teaching even by making mistakes

7. Learning / takes place / all the time

8. You / can learn / to do some things / very quickly

9. More difficult skills / such as reading or writing / can take / much longer
may require / help

10. Learning / is / a lifelong journey

11. You / will continue / to learn all kinds of things / throughout your life

12. The more / you learn // the more interesting / life / becomes

E   Grammar for Reading   pp.88~89

1. **Learning** is / the process / of **finding** out about things. 어떤 것들에 대해

2. It helps / you / **understand** the world around you.
세상을 이해하는 것을

3. **It** leads / to personal **growth** and development.
이는 이어진다(그것은 이끈다)

4. You can learn / new knowledge, skills, attitudes, **or** behaviors. 너는 배울 수 있다

5. There **are** / different ways / **to learn**.
여러 가지 방법이

6. You can learn / by experience, study, or teaching, / and even by **making** mistakes.
경험, 공부, 가르침을 통해

7. Learning **takes place** / all the time. 항상

8. You can learn / **to do** some things / very **quickly**.
매우 빠르게

9. **More difficult** skills, / such as reading or **writing**, / can take 읽기나 쓰기와 같은
much **longer** / and may / **require** / help.
필요로 할 수 있다

10. Learning **is** / a lifelong journey. 평생의 여정

11. You will continue / to learn all **kinds** of things / throughout **your** life. 너의 평생에 걸쳐

12. The **more** / you learn, / the **more** interesting / life becomes. 더 많이

Unit 14   Movement 움직임   pp.90~95

A   Speed Reading

우리는 몸을 움직여 걷고, 달리고, 스트레칭하고, 춤을 출 수 있다. 운동 신경이 뇌가 우리의 근육을 제어할 수 있게 해준다. 수천 개의 근육이 뼈에 붙어 있다. 우리가 움직이고 싶을 때 뇌는 어떤 근육이 필요한지 파악한다. 그런 다음, 뇌는 이 근육들에 신호를 보내 뼈를 움직이라고 지시한다.

인간의 뇌에는 1,000억 개 이상의 신경세포가 있다. 뇌의 앞부분은 계획을 세우고 결정을 내린다. 그것은 신경세포로부터 수신한 다양한 유형의 정보를 처리하여 이를 수행한다. 이 정보를 감각 정보라고 한다. 감각 정보는 시각, 청각, 촉각, 미각, 후각과 같은 감각에서 비롯된다.

B 　Reading for Information　　　　　　　　　　p.91

1. 1) Yes　　　2) No　　　3) No

2. 1) muscles　　　2) brain

3. sensory information

C 　Checking Vocabulary　　　　　　　　　p.91

1. ⓑ 뇌와 신체의 다른 부분 사이에서 신호를 전달하는 신체 내
부의 길고 가느다란 가닥

2. ⓐ 온몸을 통제하며 생각하고, 느끼고, 기억할 수 있게 해주
는 머릿속의 기관

3. ⓒ 움직일 때 사용하는 몸속의 부위

4. ⓔ 연결하거나 고정하거나 잇다

5. ⓓ 결심하는 행위나 그 결과

D 　Reading for Learning　　　　　　　　pp.92~93

1. You / can walk, run, stretch, and dance / by moving
your body

2. Motor nerves / allow / the brain / to control your
muscles

3. Thousands of muscles / are attached / to your bones

4. you / want / to move
your brain / figures out / which muscles are needed

5. Then / the brain / sends / messages / to these
muscles / telling them to move your bones

6. The human brain / has / more than 100 billion nerve
cells

7. The front part / of the brain / plans and makes
decisions

8. It / does / this / by processing the different types of
information / received from nerve cells

9. This information / is called / sensory information

10. It / comes / from your senses / such as sight,
hearing, touch, taste, and smell

E 　Grammar for Reading　　　　　　　　pp.94~95

1. You can walk **/ run**, stretch, and dance **/ by moving**
your body. 너의 몸을 움직여서

2. Motor nerves **allow /** the brain **/ to control** your

---

muscles. (너의) 근육을 제어하는 것을

3. Thousands of muscles **/ are** attached **/ to** your
bones. 수천 개의 근육이

4. When you want **/ to move**,
your brain **figures out /** which muscles **are** needed.
어떤 근육이 필요한지를

5. Then, **/** the brain **sends /** messages **/ to** these
muscles, 메시지를
telling **/** them **/ to move** your bones. (너의) 뼈를 움직
이라고

6. The human brain **has /** more **than** 100 billion nerve
cells. 1,000억 개 이상의

7. The front part of the brain **/ plans** and **makes**
decisions. 뇌의 앞부분은

8. It **does /** this **/** by **processing** the different types of
information 다양한 유형의 정보를
received **from** nerve **cells**.

9. This information is **called /** sensory information.
감각 정보

10. It **comes /** from your senses, **/** such as sight,
hearing, touch, taste, and smell. 너의 감각에서

Unit 15　Preteens 프리틴(사춘기 직전 아동)　pp.96~101

A 　Speed Reading

프리틴(사춘기 직전 아동)이란 9세에서 12세 사이의 아이들을 말
한다. 이 시기는 아동기와 청소년기 사이의 변화 시기이다. 프리틴
들은 보통 사춘기 초기 단계를 포함하여 중대한 육체적, 정서적 변
화를 겪는다. 그들은 자신의 외모에 더 많은 관심을 기울인다.

프리틴들은 또한 십 대가 되어 가면서 사회적 변화를 경험한다. 그
들은 부모로부터 더 독립하고 친구들과 더 많은 시간을 보낸다. 그
들은 종종 같은 성별의 또래들과 친밀한 우정을 형성한다. 프리틴
들은 또한 유명한 운동선수나 음악가, 영화배우에게 매료될 수 있
다. 그들은 자신의 정체성과 관심사, 스타일을 탐구하기 시작한다.

B 　Reading for Information　　　　　　　　p.97

1. 1) Yes　　　2) Yes　　　3) No

2. 1) puberty   2) parents

3. 신체적 변화, 감정적 변화, 사회적 변화

C Checking Vocabulary   p.97

1. ⓑ 아동기와 성인기 사이의 인생 시기

2. ⓒ 감정과 관련된, 특히 다른 사람들과의 관계 속에서 자신에 대해 어떻게 느끼는지와 관련된

3. ⓐ 신체의

4. ⓔ 다른 사람과 같은 지위나 나이대, 혹은 같은 능력을 갖춘 사람

5. ⓓ 스포츠 혹은 다른 신체 활동에 참여하는 사람

D Reading for Learning   pp.98~99

1. Preteens / are / children / between the ages of 9 and 12

2. This stage / is / the time of change / between childhood and adolescence

3. Preteens / usually / experience / significant physical and emotional changes / including the early stages of puberty

4. They / pay / more attention / to how they look

5. Preteens / also / experience / social changes
they / move / toward becoming teenagers

6. They / become / more independent / from their parents
spend / more time / with friends

7. They / often / form / close friendships / with peers of the same gender

8. Preteens / may also become fascinated / by famous athletes, musicians, or movie stars

9. They / begin / to explore their own identities, interests, and styles

E Grammar for Reading   pp.100~101

1. Preteens **are** / children / between the ages of 9 **and** 12. 9세에서 12세 사이의

2. **This** stage **is** / the time of change / between childhood and adolescence. 아동기와 청소년기 사이의

3. Preteens **usually experience** / significant physical

and emotional changes, 보통 겪는다
including the early stages of puberty. 사춘기의 초기 단계를

4. **They** pay / more attention / to **how** they look. 더 많은 관심을

5. Preteens also experience / **social** changes 사회적 변화를
as they move / **toward** becoming teenagers.

6. They **become** / more independent / **from** their parents 그들의 부모로부터
and spend / more time / with friends. 더 많은 시간을

7. They **often form** / close friendships / **with** peers of the same gender. 같은 성별의 또래들과

8. Preteens / may also **become** fascinated
by famous athletes, musicians, or movie stars. 유명한 운동선수, 음악가

9. They begin / **to explore** / their own identities, interests, and styles. 정체성, 관심사, 스타일을

Unit 16 Sickness 질병   pp.102~107

A Speed Reading

질병은 몸이나 마음이 평소처럼 잘 작동하지 않을 때 생겨나는 느낌이다. 질병은 여러 가지 이유로 발생할 수 있다. 질병은 종종 세균이라는 아주 작은 생명체에 의해 발생한다. 어떤 질병은 부모로부터 유전된다. 또 어떤 질병은 오염, 화학물질, 방사능에 의해 발생한다. 우울증이나 불안은 마음에 영향을 끼칠 수 있다.

우리 몸은 세균을 공격하기 위해서 특수 세포를 보내 세균을 물리친다. 수십억 마리의 세균이 우리의 몸 바깥에 항상 존재한다. 대부분은 무해하지만, 일부는 감기, 독감이나 홍역과 같은 질병을 일으킬 수 있다. 또 다른 세균들은 신체 일부를 아프게 할 수 있다. 몸을 청결하게 관리하면 건강을 유지하는 데 도움이 된다.

B Reading for Information   p.103

1. 1) Yes   2) No   3) Yes

2. Germs

3. 몸을 청결하게 유지하는 것

C Checking Vocabulary
p.103

1. ⓑ 신체나 정신의 건강하지 않은 상태
2. ⓐ 지구를 더럽게 만드는 것
3. ⓔ 깊은 슬픔이나 저조한 기분
4. ⓒ 해치거나 파괴하다, 해를 끼치기 시작하다
5. ⓓ 해를 끼칠 힘이나 의도가 없는

D Reading for Learning
pp.104~105

1. Sickness / is / the feeling / that occurs / when your body or mind isn't working as well as usual
2. It / can happen / for many reasons
3. Often / sickness / is caused / by tiny living things / called germs
4. Some illnesses / are inherited / from parents
5. Others / are caused / by pollution, chemicals, or radiation
6. Depression or anxiety / can affect / your mind
7. Your body / fights off / germs / by sending special cells / to attack them
8. Billions of germs / live / on the outside of your body / all the time
9. Most / are / harmless
   some / can cause / illnesses / like colds, the flu, or measles
10. Other germs / can make / parts of your body / hurt
11. Keeping your body clean / helps / you / stay healthy

E Grammar for Reading
pp.106~107

1. Sickness **is /** the feeling **/** that **occurs** 일어나는
   when **/** your body or mind **/** isn't **working /** as well
   as usual. 작동하지 않고 있다
2. It can **happen /** for many **reasons**. 여러 가지 이유로
3. Often, **/** sickness is **caused /** by tiny living things **/**
   called germs. 아주 작은 생명체에 의해
4. Some illnesses **/ are** inherited **/ from** parents.
   유전된다
5. Others are **caused /** by pollution, chemicals, or
   radiation. 방사능에 의해
6. Depression or **anxiety /** can affect **/** your mind.

7. Your body fights off / germs / by **sending** special cells / to **attack** them. 그들(세균)을 공격하기 위해
8. Billions of **germs** / live / on the outside of your body / all the **time**. 항상
9. Most **are** / harmless,
   but some can cause **/ illnesses** / like colds, the flu, or measles. 감기, 독감이나 홍역과 같은
10. **Other** germs / can make / parts of your body / **hurt**.
    네 신체 일부를
11. **Keeping** your body clean / **helps** / you / stay healthy. 건강을 유지하는 데

Unit 17 Spiders 거미
pp.108~113

A Speed Reading

거미는 곤충이 아니다. 거미는 6개가 아닌 8개 다리를 가지고 있다. 거미는 모양과 색깔이 다양하다. 거미는 어둠 속에서도 볼 수 있는 특별한 눈과 주변 환경을 감지할 수 있는 아주 작은 털들이 다리에 있다. 대부분의 거미는 인간에게 무해하며 해충을 잡아먹음으로써 해충 방제에 도움이 된다.

대부분의 거미는 곤충을 먹지만, 어떤 거미들은 개구리, 물고기, 작은 동물을 먹고 산다. 모든 거미는 끈적끈적한 비단실을 뽑아낸다. 이 비단실은 거미가 올라가거나 위험을 피하도록 돕는 안전 밧줄 역할을 한다. 거미는 또한 먹이를 잡고 감싸기 위한 거미줄을 만드는 데 비단실을 사용한다. 거미들은 보금자리를 만들고 알을 보호한다.

B Reading for Information
p.109

1. 1) No   2) No   3) Yes
2. 1) six   2) eight   3) silk
3. 거미는 해충을 잡아먹는다.

C Checking Vocabulary
p.109

1. ⓒ 또 다른 동물에게 잡아먹히는 동물
2. ⓓ 감각을 통해 느끼거나 경험하다
3. ⓐ 농작물에 손해를 끼치는, 혹은 해로운 곤충이나 동물

4. ⓔ 벗어나거나 자유롭게 되다, 붙잡히거나 해를 입는 것을 피하다

5. ⓑ 거미가 벌레를 잡기 위해 만드는 것

D pp.110~111

1. Spiders / are not / insects

2. They / have / eight legs / instead of six

3. They / come / in many shapes and colors

4. They / have / special eyes / to see in the dark
tiny hairs / on their legs / to sense their surroundings

5. Most spiders / are / harmless / to humans
help / control pests / by eating them

6. most spiders / eat / insects
some / feed on / frogs, fish, and small animals

7. All spiders / spin / sticky silk threads

8. The silk / acts / as a safety rope
helping / them / climb or escape danger

9. Spiders / also / use / silk / to build webs / for
catching and wrapping prey

10. They / make / nests
protect / their eggs

E Grammar for Reading pp.112~113

1. Spiders **are** not / insects. 곤충이

2. **They** have / eight **legs** / instead of six. 8개의 다리를

3. They **come** / in **many** shapes and colors. 다양한 모양과

4. They have / special eyes / **to see** in the dark 어둠 속에서
and tiny hairs / **on** their legs / **to sense** their surroundings. 그들의 다리에

5. Most **spiders** are / harmless / to humans 인간에게
and **help** / control pests / by **eating** them. 그것들을 잡아먹음으로써

6. **While** most spiders **eat** / insects,
some **feed on** / frogs, **fish**, and small animals. 일부는 먹고 산다

7. All **spiders** spin / sticky silk threads. 모든 거미는 뽑아낸다

8. The silk **acts** / as a safety rope, / **helping** / **them** /

climb or escape danger. 안전 밧줄로서

9. Spiders also use / silk / **to build** webs / for **catching**
and wrapping prey. 먹이를 잡고 감싸기 위한

10. They make / nests / and **protect** / their eggs. 보금자리를

Unit 18 Teens 십 대(청소년) pp.114~119

A Speed Reading

십 대(청소년)는 더 이상 어린이가 아니다. 그들은 사춘기 동안 급격한 신체적 성장과 변화를 경험한다. 십 대가 된다는 것은 새로운 몸을 얻는 것과 같다. 대부분의 십 대들에게는 외모가 중요해진다. 우정과 또래 관계도 더욱 중요해진다. 이 단계는 성장과 발견으로 가득하다.

십 대들은 세상에 대해 배우기를 열망한다. 그들은 처음으로 주변의 어른 없이 스스로 무언가를 할 수 있다. 그들은 한계를 시험하고 새로운 경험을 추구할 수도 있다. 고도의 사고 능력을 개발하면서 자신의 정체성을 탐구하게 된다. 이러한 변화를 겪는 동안 강렬한 감정과 기분 변화는 흔하게 일어난다.

B Reading for Information p.115

1. 1) No   2) Yes   3) Yes

2. 1) body   2) physical

3. 강렬한 감정과 기분 변화가 흔히 발생한다.

C Checking Vocabulary p.115

1. ⓑ 짧은 시간 내에 일어나는, 빠르게 움직이는

2. ⓐ 사람이나 사물들이 서로 연결되는 방식

3. ⓓ 어떤 일을 하고 싶어 매우 흥분하고 관심이 많은, 몹시 원하는

4. ⓔ 두 개의 사물이나 영역을 구분하는 선이나 경계

5. ⓒ 사람의 감정들이 빠르게 변화하는 것

D Reading for Learning pp.116~117

1. Teenagers / are / no longer children

2. During puberty / they / experience / rapid physical
growth and changes

3. Becoming a teenager / is / like getting a new body

4. Looking good / becomes / important / to most teens

5. Friendships and peer relationships / also / become /
   more important

6. This stage / is / full / of growth and discovery

7. Teenagers / are / eager / to learn about the world

8. For the first time / they / can do / things / on their
   own / without any adults around

9. They / may test / boundaries
   seek / new experiences

10. they / develop / advanced thinking skills
    they / explore / their identity

11. Strong emotions and mood swings / are / common
    they / navigate / these changes

E **Grammar for Reading**   pp.118~119

1. Teenagers are / no longer **children**.
   더 이상 어린이가 아닌

2. **During** puberty, / they experience / rapid physical
   growth and changes. 사춘기 동안

3. **Becoming** a teenager is / like **getting** a new body.
   새로운 몸을 얻는 것과

4. **Looking** good **becomes** / important / to most
   teens. 대부분의 십 대들에게

5. Friendships and peer relationships / also **become** /
   more important. 더욱 중요한

6. This stage is / **full** / **of** growth and **discovery**.
   성장과 발견

7. Teenagers are / eager / **to learn** about the world.
   세상에 대해

8. For the first **time**, / they can do / things / on their
   own / **without** any adults around. 처음으로

9. They **may** test / boundaries / and **seek** / new
   experiences. 시험할 수도 있다

10. As **they** develop / advanced thinking skills,
    they **explore** / their identity. 자신들의 정체성을

11. Strong emotions and mood swings / **are** / common
    강한 감정과 기분 변화는
    as they navigate / **these** changes. 이러한 변화들을

Volcanoes 화산
pp.120~125

A **Speed Reading**

우리 발 아래의 땅은 단단한 듯 보이지만 어떤 곳은 약하거나 갈라져 있다. 이런 약한 지점들이 화산이 형성되는 곳이다. 화산은 지각에 난 구멍이다. 이 구멍을 통해 녹은 암석, 화산재, 가스가 분출된다. 지각 아래의 녹은 암석을 마그마라고 한다. 마그마가 화산에서 흘러나올 때, 그것을 용암이라고 한다.

용암은 때때로 붉고 뜨거운 강처럼 매우 빠르게 이동할 수 있다. 화산은 보통 원뿔 모양의 산으로, 굳어진 용암으로 형성된다. 그러나 화산은 다양한 모양과 크기로 전 세계 곳곳에서 발견된다. 화산 분출은 지구의 지형을 형성하는 데 중요한 역할을 한다.

B **Reading for Information**   p.121

1. 1) No   2) Yes   3) No

2. 1) Magma   2) lava

3. 녹은 암석, 화산재, 가스

C **Checking Vocabulary**   p.121

1. ⓓ 단단한 형태를 가진, 액체나 기체가 아닌

2. ⓐ 화산에서 나오는 뜨겁고 녹은 암석

3. ⓑ 얼음이 물로 변하는 것처럼 열로 인해 고체에서 액체로
   변하다

4. ⓔ 단단하거나 딱딱하게 된

5. ⓒ 어떤 것이나 누군가를 어떤 장소에서 강제로 내보내다

D **Reading for Learning**   pp.122~123

1. The ground / under your feet / seems / solid
   in some places / it / is / weak or cracked

2. These weak spots / are / where volcanoes form

3. A volcano / is / an opening / in the Earth's crust.

4. Through this opening / melted rock, ash, and gases /
   are expelled

5. The melted rock / beneath the Earth's crust / is
   called / magma

6. it / flows / out of a volcano
   it / is called / lava

---

7. Lava / can sometimes move / very fast / like a red-hot river

8. Volcanoes / are / often / cone-shaped mountains / formed from hardened lava

9. However / they / come / in many shapes and sizes are found / all over the world

10. Volcanic eruptions / play / a key role / in shaping the Earth's landscape

---

E **Grammar for Reading**   pp.124~125

1. The ground / under your feet / **seems** / solid, 네 발 아래

but in some **places**, / it is / weak or cracked. 어떤 곳에서는

2. **These** weak spots **are** / where volcanoes form. 화산이 형성되는

3. A volcano is / **an** opening / in the Earth's crust. 지각

4. Through this opening, / **melted** rock, ash, and gases / **are** expelled. 이 구멍을 통해

5. The melted rock / **beneath** the Earth's crust / **is** called / magma. 녹은 암석은

6. When it **flows** / out of a volcano, / it **is** called / lava. 화산 밖으로

7. Lava can sometimes **move** / very fast, / like a red-hot river. 붉고 뜨거운 강처럼

8. Volcanoes **are often** / cone-shaped mountains, 원뿔 모양의 산

formed from **hardened** lava.

9. However, / **they come** / in many shapes and **sizes** 다양한 모양과 크기로

and are **found** / all over the world. 전 세계 곳곳에서

10. Volcanic eruptions **play** / a key role / in **shaping** the Earth's landscape. 중요한 역할을

A **Speed Reading**

물은 우리 주변 어디에나 있다. 대부분은 지구 표면의 약 3분의 2를 덮고 있는 바다와 대양에서 발견된다. 물은 또한 땅과 대기에도 존재한다. 추운 곳에서 물은 얼음과 눈으로 얼어 있다. 지하에서는 토양과 암석에 저장되어 있다. 공기 중에서 물은 눈에 보이지 않는 기체가 된다.

모든 물은 재순환된다. 물은 지구의 대기와 지표면, 지하를 통해 이동한다. 태양이 바다를 데우면 물은 수증기로 변해 공기 중으로 올라가서 구름을 형성한다. 바람이 그 구름을 대지 위로 데려오는데, 여기서 물이 비나 눈으로 내린다. 빗물은 개울과 강으로 흘러 마침내 바다로 돌아간다. 그러면 순환이 처음부터 다시 시작된다.

B **Reading for Information**   p.127

1. 1) Yes   2) No   3) No

2. 1) recycled   2) underground

3. rain, snow

C **Checking Vocabulary**   p.127

1. ⓒ 땅이나 물 같은 것의 맨 위층

2. ⓓ 미래에 사용하기 위해 모아두다

3. ⓑ 보이지 않는

4. ⓔ 어떤 것을 새로운 방식으로 다시 사용하다

5. ⓐ 끓는 물에서 나오는 김 같은, 공기 중의 아주 작은 물방울

D **Reading for Learning**   pp.128~129

1. Water / is / all around us

2. Most of it / is found / in seas and oceans / which cover about two-thirds of Earth's surface

3. Water / also / exists / in the ground and the air

4. In cold places / it / is frozen / as ice and snow

5. Underground / it / is stored / in the soil and rocks

6. In the air / it / becomes / an invisible gas

7. All water / is recycled

8. It / moves / through the Earth's atmosphere, surface, and underground

9. the sun / warms / the oceans

water / turns / into vapor / rising into the air to form clouds

10. Wind / carries / the clouds / over the land / where the water falls as rain or snow

11. Rainwater / flows / into streams and rivers / finally returning to the oceans

12. Then / the cycle / begins / all over again

E　**Grammar for Reading**　　　　pp.130~131

1. Water **is** / all around **us**. 우리 주변 어디에든

2. **Most** of it **/ is found** / in seas and oceans, 발견된다
which cover / about **two-thirds** of Earth's surface.
약 3분의 2를

3. Water also **exists** / in the ground and the air.
땅과 대기에도

4. In cold places, **/ it** is frozen / as **ice** and **snow**.
얼어 있다

5. Underground, **/ it is stored** / in the soil and **rocks**.
저장되어 있다

6. In the air, **/ it becomes / an** invisible gas. 공기 중에서

7. All **water** / is recycled. 재순환된다

8. It **moves** / through the Earth's atmosphere, surface,
and underground. 지하를 통해

9. When **the sun** warms / the oceans, 바다를
water **turns** / into vapor, **/ rising** into the air **/** to
form clouds. 수증기로

10. **Wind** carries / the clouds **/ over** the land,
바람이 운반한다
where / the water **falls** / as rain or snow. 비나 눈으로

11. Rainwater **flows** / into streams and rivers, **/** finally
returning / to the oceans. 빗물은 흐른다

12. Then, / the cycle **begins** / all over again. 순환이 시작
된다